Presented To

From

Date

100
WORST BOSSES

*Learning from the Very Worst
How to be Your
Very Best*

By Jim Stovall

Published by Companion Enterprises, Inc., 5840 South Memorial Drive, Suite #312, Tulsa, OK 74145-9082

Companion Enterprises, Inc. books may be purchased in bulk for educational, business, fundraising, or sales promotional use. For information email *jim@jimstovall.com* or call 918-627-1000.

Library of Congress Cataloging-in-Publication Data

Stovall, Jim

100 Worst Bosses: Learning from the Very Worst How to be Your Very Best / by Jim Stovall

1. Business 2. Success 3. Personal Development

13 digit ISBN: 978-0-9672427-1-2 (hardcover)
10 digit ISBN: 0-9672427-1-1

Printed in the United States of America

10 11 12 13 14   8 7 6 5 4 3 2

Jacket by Judy McHenry – Tulsa, OK
Interior layout/design by Liquid Lotus, LLC –
Colorado Springs, CO

DEDICATION

This book is dedicated to the wonderful people at Express Employment Professionals. They not only facilitated the gathering of *100 Worst Bosses* stories, they have helped countless people find great jobs, great careers, and great bosses. This book is also dedicated to Tim Tomlinson and his team at Global Procurement Solutions. They have printed and distributed many of my books, including this one, making me look better than I deserve. And, finally, as always, this book is dedicated to Dorothy Thompson who takes my words and crafts them into the sentences, paragraphs, and chapters that you hold in your hands.

TABLE OF CONTENTS

FOREWORD

In the staffing industry, we get an inside look at tens of thousands of different companies. Since opening our doors in 1983, we've seen the good, the bad, and the ugly. Thankfully, the fact that you're reading this book and looking for answers about leadership probably puts you in the "good" category. It is our belief that people work for people, not for companies. Therefore, we can utilize a book such as this to further enhance our leadership skills. That's why we were excited to help Jim collect stories to create this book. We were inspired when Jim spoke at our regional conference, touched by his book *The Ultimate Gift*, and improved our work habits with *Ultimate Productivity*, so we were elated at the opportunity to partner with Jim throughout this endeavor.

While reading the stories in the book may make you pat yourself on the back for not being as bad as these bosses, stop and take a close look at their behavior to see if you have any similar tendencies that you may need to correct. For example, are you known for being grumpy in the morning? Do employees avoid saying "hello" or meeting with you during the first few hours of the

day? If so, maybe you need to make an effort to be a little friendlier in the mornings even if you're not a morning person.

So, as you read, laugh, and cringe, see what you can learn about yourself. How can you become an even stronger leader? And, when you're finished, pass the book on to your employees to show them how good they really have it.

Robert A. Funk
CEO and Founder
Express Employment Professionals

CHAPTER ONE

The Hunt for The Worst Bosses

There are very few bad
children, pets, or employees.
There are just bad parents,
pet owners, and bosses.

I've written over a dozen books. They have been translated into more than 30 languages, and several of them have been made or are being made into movies. Every book creates unique challenges and struggles. This one has certainly lived up to that.

In the past, I have written books such as *Success Secrets of Super Achievers* which highlights dozens of successful people who are at the very top of their field in business, sports, politics, or entertainment. When I decided to chronicle the exploits of the *100 Worst Bosses*, it presented some interesting challenges. First, I had to define what a bad boss is, and secondly, I had to go find them.

On the surface, defining a bad boss is relatively easy. If we are rating movies, dining experiences, or vacation travel, opinions will differ on which particular film, meal, or trip is the very best. But when we suffer through a bad movie, meal, or trip, we can all agree on what constitutes a bad one.

As we will learn through the ensuing chapters, a great boss provides leadership, direction, critique, and a positive example which allows each employee to fulfill their potential while serving the organization.

A bad boss would be one who fails in at least one of these areas, but to be immortalized as one of the worst bosses, you've got to create an environment so toxic that none of these elements are present or they are overshadowed by the deficiencies to such an extent that employees are unable to approach their potential or even function.

In the distant past, I have had some jobs that might be considered less than ideal. I have washed dishes in an Italian restaurant, delivered newspapers in the freezing rain, and dug ditches in 100 degree heat. Even these types of jobs can be fulfilling if there is a positive work environment. This positive work environment is primarily provided by the boss.

If you will think of the most enjoyable weekend or evening you have ever spent, you will realize that the level of your satisfaction is created more by the people you are with than what you're doing or where you're doing it. I would rather go to a mediocre fast food restaurant with someone I enjoy than go to a Five Star restaurant with someone who is obnoxious.

Bosses set the tone and create the conditions in a work environment. It is more desirable to perform a menial, mundane job for a great boss than to get your dream job and be saddled with a bad boss.

Being a worst boss is not simply about differing personalities or work styles. In a previous book, *Ultimate Productivity*, I explored how all of us function uniquely in the areas of motivation, communication, and implementation. Once we understand our unique traits and the differences among the people with whom we work, we can function as a very successful team.

My colleagues and I developed a Productivity Profile which helps any employee or employer discover their strengths with respect to motivation, communication, and implementation. If you or your colleagues would like to take this Productivity Profile at no cost and receive your individualized assessment, simply go to *www.UltimateProductivity.com* and enter your access code: 586404. I feel very fortunate to be able to give you this gift which could be a key to unlocking the greatness within you and everyone with whom you work.

Regardless of your strengths, weaknesses, and preferences, a worst boss makes it impossible to function. You will read their stories within these pages. These stories are true and are shared from the perspective and in the words of real employees who worked for these worst bosses. I want to thank everyone around the world who submitted a worst boss story and the great people at

Express Employment Professionals who helped us compile the submissions. There were many more than 100 stories submitted, and there are less than 100 stories in this book as some have been combined.

The names of people, places, and organizations have been altered to protect the innocent or, more likely, to protect the guilty; however, in every case, these stories recount the real experiences of real people, just like you and me.

You will find some of the stories shocking, others sad, and many are actually humorous. It is not my intent to ridicule any of the bad bosses; however, for all the pain that has been suffered at their hands, I think you and I are at least entitled to a good laugh now and then.

I have identified the various types of worst bosses with animals. At this point, I would like to apologize to any snakes, rats, or weasels who may be reading this book, as I realize it is offensive for them to be identified with the worst bosses.

Beyond simply sharing *Worst Bosses* stories, I want you to learn the tips and techniques that are included in each chapter so that the next time you are confronted with a worst boss, you can take action.

I hope you will continue to seek the very best in bosses and career opportunities. There will be updates and tools available to you at *www.WorstBosses.com.*

Most people not only have a boss but, to someone in the organization, they are a boss. When you and I think of bad boss experiences we have had in the past, we think of other people and likely never ourselves.

When you read the final page of this book, I want you to be empowered to never again suffer the frustration and indignity of having a worst boss and, maybe more importantly, I want you to resolve to never again exhibit any of the traits of being a bad boss yourself.

Most of us spend more time with the people at work than we do our family, friends, and loved ones. It is not imperative that we have a friendship with our boss or with everyone with whom we work; however, if we are going to be fulfilled in our work life, it is imperative that we have mutual respect, communication, and understanding with our boss and colleagues.

Statistics tell us that 85% of people do not enjoy their job. This is to say that if they won the lottery or their long lost rich uncle died, leaving them wealthy, they would never darken the door of their employer again. This is sad, because among life's great pleasures is that of doing a job well and making a difference in the world, while being recognized, fairly compensated, and appreciated for your efforts.

If you are currently in a job where you do not experience this sort of satisfaction, it is likely due, in large part or in whole, to a bad boss. As you read this book, resolve to make the changes in yourself and your environment that will allow you to enjoy your work while increasing your value to the organization. If you're not able to make the changes necessary to bring fulfillment to your work life, resolve to begin taking steps that will result in you finding a new job or career where you can flourish.

Unfortunately, worst bosses are not unique or rare. Virtually everyone I contacted has a worst boss story. Since worst bosses are not going to become extinct at any time in the near future, you and I need to learn how to deal with them and succeed.

The Hunt for The Worst Bosses

CHAPTER TWO

The Rat

**Some bosses simply need
polishing on the surface
while others are rotten to
the core.**

There is probably no creature more maligned and loathed in our world today than the lowly rat. You can dress it up or try to make it cute and color- ful, but it's still just a rat. Rats are distasteful, dis- gusting, and even dangerous. They carry and spread many diseases.

Some bosses are in need of fine tuning or some simple adjustments in demeanor, communication, or boundaries. Rat bosses are simply the worst of everything. They create a toxic, intolerable environ- ment that must be changed immediately. If you have a rat boss, your proverbial employment house is on fire. This is an emergency! You must either put the fire out immediately or get out now.

A Canadian woman found this out the hard way.

Well, it all began when my boss was promoted into a position that he was neither qualified nor suited for. The position: Director, Human Resources. The problem: This guy had absolutely no tact, diplomacy, or professionalism about him.

He would yell when he was angry, lie to employees with a straight face, take products the company made for his own personal use, and on top of it all he wanted to sit and tell me about people in the company and their relationships they had had (complete with details of when and where), and whenever he could he always sat really close to you or would lean over you. He was a jerk and a creep all rolled into one.

One day after he had been hauled in his boss's office for something he had done, he came back to our office and an hour later asked me to come into his office. He proceeded to walk around the office swinging a Louisville Slugger baseball bat while I sat in the chair. I can't even remember the topic of the conversation. All I remember was he was upset, and he wanted to intimidate me. All I kept thinking was, "You are a dangerous idiot! How is it nobody else sees this?"

There are very few workplace behaviors that are inappropriate in absolutely all situations. The most drastic action or unusual behavior might be deemed appropriate in a very narrow and unique circumstance; however, I think we can all agree that unless you are Albert Pujols or another major league baseball player, swinging a bat in the workplace is totally unacceptable.

There are certain bad boss activities such as swinging a baseball bat in anger that are so egregious and out of bounds that you simply have to immediately and clearly state, for the record—hopefully in the presence of witnesses—that you will never tolerate this behavior, not even for a minute. If your statement is greeted with anything other than absolute acceptance, you should head for the nearest exit immediately and mail in your letter of resignation.

I had thought a baseball bat had to be the worst weapon utilized by a rat boss until we received the following story from a woman in North Carolina.

I worked for the owner and CEO of a marketing firm in North Carolina. He is a multi-millionaire who has everything that money can buy but not happiness. He is a miserable man that takes it out on everyone. There was not a day that went by that he did not call each of us a stupid idiot. He always made one of us sit in his office and watch whenever he fired another employee, just to intimidate everyone.

My co-worker and girlfriend finally quit 6 months ago after he held up a gun and said he was going to shoot her if she didn't balance the books. After she quit, he tried to sue her for embezzlement.

Some actions of bad bosses are rude, ill-advised, or merely bad business practices, while others that involve baseball bats and guns brandished in anger are simply inhumane and criminal. There is no excuse and no alternative. You must get out of these types of rat boss situations.

Other rat bosses may not threaten your life directly, but their incompetence can put everyone's health, safety, and life at risk.

During my career as a firefighter at one of the larger metropolitan fire departments, I had the misfortune of working under an Assistant Fire Chief that was not only overbearing, obnoxious, and belittling but was a perfect example of the misuse of authority.

The following is a partial list of some of his less desirable traits:

1. He thrived on using his authority to limit discussion to only one opinion, his own. If anyone appeared to question him, he would promptly and loudly exert his authority over them and chastise them into submission. We all did our best to avoid any contact with him. Example: As happened several times, if he heard firefighters discussing any vehicle, other than a Chevrolet pickup, he would immediately stop their conversation, by angrily yelling at them, and chastise every firefighter in that discussion. As a point of interest, on his days off, he sold used Chevrolet pickups.

2. He would not allow new or improved firefighting procedures to be discussed or enacted, other than when he was ordered to do so by the Fire Chief or the City Manager. Since firefighters constantly attend training schools across the country, suggesting an educated improvement was a sure way to receive retribution. He called improvements unnecessary and stupid. As another point of interest, he was the most uneducated man on the department. Example: He was afraid of fire and would often hide behind the fire truck at a fire scene. His shift had more injuries, due to his bad judgment calls, than all of the other shifts combined.

3. He used his position as Assistant Fire Chief for personal financial advantage. Example: He would ask firefighters to work for free, on his own personal property, on their days off. We were all afraid to say no because he had the power to terminate our employment if he so chose. He used his power to intimidate firefighters into doing what he wanted while risking our lives.

The incompetence and arrogance of a rat boss can be as dangerous as a loaded gun. This eventually will result in pain, suffering, death, and destruction. There is no alternative other than to sound the alarm and evacuate.

Beyond the physical threats to life and limb of rat bosses who are angered or incompetent, there are rat bosses who take advantage of their power to victimize the most vulnerable among us.

Young people can gain confidence, people skills, and real world experience on their first job unless, of course, they encounter a rat boss.

I was working at a fast food restaurant as a teenager. My boss was an older man. He was a bachelor at about 43 and loved to share his sexual frustrations with his employees. One day in particular, he was discussing his marital status, so I in turn asked when he was actually going to get married. I was clearly underage and he replied with, "Are you 18 yet? Exactly. Looks like it'll be a few years."

Not only was he degrading to his employees by exposing his love life, he also talked about his non-existent sex life and how he fulfilled himself. My boss also had an extreme anger problem. His mood would change in a matter of seconds, and it only took the smallest thing to push him over the edge. Once he became frustrated, he would yell the most extreme profane things I've ever heard. I learned more ways to use the f word at that job than I have anywhere else.

He also owned the restaurant so he used his power to take advantage of teenage employees.

Worst first job experience EVER!

When we examine the true-life stories of rat bosses, they seem so outrageous and absurd on the outside looking in that we wonder why mature adults or those parents responsible for minor children don't terminate the employment experience immediately and flee. As anyone who has been in any of these situations would tell you, it's often not that simple.

Statistics tell us that 25% of Americans have less than a two-week cash reserve, and 50% have less than a one-month cushion. This type of financial pressure can keep you in a cage with the most obnoxious, destructive, and dangerous rat boss.

If you want to have sufficient rat traps and a perimeter of rat poison protecting your work life and career, keep your resume updated, and start building an emergency account which contains six months of your living expenses.

There's no bigger life or career emergency than dealing daily with a rat boss, but if you have your resume updated and your six-month cash reserve ready, you can simply spring the rat trap, find the nearest exit, and head for greener pastures.

CHAPTER THREE

The Weasel

Honesty and integrity are
the foundations of
everything good.

Throughout literature and recorded history, the weasel is depicted as a conniving, scheming thief. I know that weasels will take eggs from bird nests or chicken coops, but compared to some of the weasel boss stories I received, they are angelic.

Few things are more frustrating in an employment situation than realizing, in the midst of your hard work, you are involved in something dishonest, illegal, or dishonorable.

I was hired to restructure a financially failing medical practice. The original partners held one another accountable. Then the senior partner got sick, and one doctor took over. He moved money from his partners, hiring a personal buddy for an accountant, who was glad to play along. They joked about getting rid of the senior partner, the inability of one partner to understand any financial statements, another's fear of talking business unpleasantness, and they repeatedly recalculated earnings. They sent fraudulent information to an insurance company paying disability payments and drove the best doctors in the practice away.

When I discussed this with the rest of the physicians, he fired me, and has blacklisted me by telling people I took money from the practice. Hardly. When the practice was unable to pay bills, I spent my own money to cover bills.

He is still in business, a leader who abuses staff and is one of the most dishonest, underhanded bosses I ever had.

Weasel bosses can not only affect your current job but your next one as well. You become vulnerable simply by being a part of an unscrupulous organization. Since the weasel boss controls the accounting, banking, and financial reporting, he not only can manipulate the numbers but the responsibility. Unless you act swiftly and decisively when the misdealings are finally exposed to the light of day, you may find that the proverbial finger of blame is pointing at you.

My boss, who was hardly ever there, kept yelling at me because our company was continually asked for C.O.D. checks instead of being granted credit accounts with our vendors. She blamed it on me, saying I didn't submit the correct information. She said I was irresponsible for not following up on why we had no credit—and so on and so on.

One day she was called out of a meeting because she needed to go to the bank and get a C.O.D. check. Before walking out, she yelled at me and said, "I can't believe you are so stupid and don't know how to fill out a credit application. I can't believe it's not approved yet. You are responsible for my wasted time."

So I picked up the phone and called the vendor, and asked what was taking so long to get our company set up with credit.

They said, "Well it's just that your company has horrible credit. The owners, themselves, do not have good enough credit to set up an account with us."

I asked if we could use a company credit card. They said, "No. Only COD or pay cash at the distribution center."

When I told my boss about the vendor's decision, her expression was priceless!

Weasel bosses want to make their financial impropriety or irresponsibility everyone else's problem. It is virtually impossible for a dedicated, hardworking, and honest employee of a weasel boss to survive.

Weasel bosses not only lie to vendors, bankers, and accountants, they lie to upper management. A salesman in Colorado found this out the hard way.

A former sales manager boss was desperate for next-day qualified prospect reporting. Sales were exceptionally slow due to an economic downturn. He told me I had better go to the local graveyard that night and bring in some solid names the next morning—no questions!

I've heard of cold sales leads, but this is ridiculous.

It is important to remember that in virtually any organization the number one expense is payroll. You don't need to steal a company's money or merchandise to be a thief. You simply need to steal an employee's time, effort, or energy.

It is important for all of us to remember that any time we don't give an honest day's work for an honest day's pay, we are stealing from our boss, our company, or the stockholders. Many employees who would never consider taking so much as an ink pen, toner cartridge, or ream of copy paper home with them, habitually waste an hour or two a day conducting personal business, goofing off, or daydreaming.

The phrase "Time is money" is certainly true when it comes to the relationship between you and your boss. In reviewing the myriad of worst bosses stories submitted as a part of this project, there were numerous stories of weasel bosses stealing from their company by using employees' time, effort, and energy for their own benefit.

Employees were compelled by weasel bosses to move furniture, do landscaping, program computers, do homework for children, and any number of other misuses of company resources.

This story is representative of those weasel boss stories.

I'm submitting a worst boss story because this boss, in my opinion, was dishonest and took advantage of his position.

This manager was known throughout our organization for "building" his house from the ground up. Everyone talked about his amazing log cabin with its huge deck and outdoor fireplace. What I found out after the fact is that the house was built by the guys who worked for him.

Now, the thing to understand is that we were a computer support department for a large oil company! And that the construction was mostly performed during work hours! Many of the guys who "volunteered" to help out on the "project" told me that they did not feel that they could say no to the boss. They worried that their jobs would be in jeopardy if they did not work at the construction site at some point.

To this day, I do not believe that upper management knew how this manager's house was actually constructed. He was later promoted and relocated to our second largest office in Houston.

When confronted with a weasel boss or rumor of a weasel boss, it is important to first and foremost document the indiscretion. Something that may look inappropriate could possibly have a logical explanation or have been approved by management.

Once you have documented the situation and if, indeed, it is dishonest, dishonorable, or illegal, you've got to choose your next steps very carefully. It is important to never directly accuse your boss of anything. You simply want to pose questions or point out possible inconsistencies.

You would not want to say, "Mr. Weasel Boss, I know you're stealing money, products, or employees' time from this company." You simply want to pose a question. "Mr. Weasel Boss, it appears that certain resources are unaccounted for. Can you point me in the right direction regarding this matter?"

Your question will meet with hostility from a guilty weasel boss, but at least you asked the question so that when you go to the accountants, lawyers, or upper management, you have stayed within the chain of command.

Although such an action threatens your job, it is important to realize that you have absolutely nothing to lose. If your career is based on working for a weasel boss in an organization of weasels, it's better to know now than later, and either fix the problem or move on immediately.

There are enough difficult issues in the dynamic between employers and employees without having to constantly question the fundamentals of honesty, legality, and integrity.

CHAPTER FOUR

The Bear

Anger often begins as a
symptom to a greater
issue, but then it can grow
to overshadow the original
problem.

Bears are thought of as cute, cuddly, and adorable creatures. They have been immortalized as teddy bears, Winnie the Pooh, Smokey the Bear, and many others. Bears can seem docile and lethargic. They even hibernate, sleeping through a significant part of the calendar year; however, there are few images more terrifying and dangerous than an angry bear.

Michelle, or Mikki as she preferred, was nearly impossible to please. Her work standards changed every day. On Monday, she'd be perfectly content if you let her know you were finished and went on your way. But come Tuesday, if you did the same thing, she'd flip out on you and jump down your throat for thinking that you were too good to have your work checked. Then she'd nit-pick your work and point out mistakes, things she had never been concerned with before.

On top of all the roller-coastering she did with work requirements, she also constantly played favorites. She'd let others go home early, or do the easy jobs or be lazy or stand around and talk just because she felt like it. Heaven forbid you speak to your coworkers if you weren't her favorite for that shift.

Working under her management was extremely stressful and a constant guessing game of how an employee should do their job. I felt defeated every night after putting in 8 hours of dedicated effort. I'm definitely a people pleaser and never being able to make her happy was really difficult.

I worked with Mikki for a year and a half, and after leaving that job I stepped into a supervisory position. One of the very first things I did after being put into management at my new job was to write down all the things I would never do to my subordinates. Mikki sure taught me a lot about how to be a bad manager. I hope no one under my supervision can ever say the same about me.

All of us become angry at some point. It is simply a matter of how we channel and control our anger. Angry bear bosses tend to be docile and hibernate a lot of the time, and then, for unpredictable and even unknown reasons, they explode.

This type of anger kills creativity and constructive criticism. Choosing to let the hibernating bear sleep, employees are unwilling to stick their neck out with a thought, idea, or suggestion.

Then there are some angry bear bosses who just take the hibernating thing too far.

A woman in Australia experienced this.

When I was very young, I worked as a receptionist/vet nurse at a five doc veterinarian hospital. The owner and doctor of the clinic was a very grumpy person. The only way I could get him to come in to work in the morning was to go to his home which was next door to the clinic with a cup of coffee and knock on the front door a few times. When he didn't answer, I would go in and then knock on his bedroom door. When he still didn't answer, I actually had to go into his bedroom and shake him, yelling his name at the same time till he finally woke up. He then proceeded to yell abuse at me for waking him. I would put the coffee down at his bedside and run back to the clinic. He was an extremely bad tempered man.

Often after I had gone into his home and proceeded into his bedroom to wake him, he would simply roll over and go back to sleep. Then I would have to go back again. This happened virtually every day I worked there.

No surprises I only lasted 5 weeks.

Angry bear bosses feel the freedom to spread their venom throughout the workplace, unchallenged. They feel very little, if any, threat of reprisal or confrontation.

As a blind person myself, you'll be happy to know that I do not drive an automobile; therefore, I have a lot of time to observe the habits of other drivers. I am always fascinated when drivers become extremely angered and yell at one another for not signaling or failing to accelerate fast enough when a light turns green.

These drivers would never display the same type of anger if they confronted one another face-to-face, but they feel a sense of isolation and become bulletproof to anger when inside the safe confines of their automobile.

Angry bear bosses feel the same way due to their power, position, and control.

My worst boss was a Jekyll & Hyde type person because you never knew which personality to expect. He had a hair trigger temper and would explode with no warning. During one of these explosions, he would generally swear at the person on the receiving end of his anger and make very demeaning statements about them with little or no basis in fact.

At times, the person involved wasn't present but he would order that they were not to work for our department again and they were black balled for reasons known only to him. When he cooled down, he might act as if nothing

had ever happened or would maintain his vendetta against the individual and treat them poorly.

His highly inappropriate behavior kept everyone on edge and created a very poor working environment. We lost valuable and competent staff members who chose not to work in such an environment. After many outbursts over a period of years, management finally removed him and the climate changed dramatically!

You've probably heard it said of someone that "They can brighten up a whole room when they walk in." As the previous story illustrates, there are some angry bear bosses that can brighten up a whole room or an entire work environment simply by leaving.

You can't fight an angry bear boss on their own terms. They are judge, jury, and executioner. This doesn't mean that you can't take some positive steps.

If you are in a position where you are forced to deal with an angry bear boss, you need to stay calm and implement the three Ds: Delay, Deflect, and Diffuse.

Most angry bear bosses only expose their angry side a small percentage of the time. If you can simply delay the confrontation, invariably you will find a more sunny disposition another hour or another day. You will still have the original issue to deal with, but you can get past the violent anger.

If you are unable to delay, you should try to deflect the anger. Calmly deal with the facts surrounding the issue at hand. Avoid the temptation to get into a shouting match or personal comments.

Finally, if you're unable to delay or deflect, and you're still feeling the heat of the angry bear boss, try to diffuse the situation. If other witnesses can be present, the angry bear boss is more likely to consider his tone and demeanor. If you can take notes or repeat some of their vile, angry language back to them calmly, often they will begin to understand the absurdity of their anger.

All of us deal with anger. This includes our own as well as friends, family, and coworkers; however, if you are forced to deal with an angry bear boss, it is a different dynamic. You never really win an argument with an angry bear boss. At a later date and time when you're most vulnerable, you will simply discover that the argument has been resumed.

Dealing with an angry bear boss is like considering a nuclear war. The only way you win is to not play the game at all.

CHAPTER FIVE

The Ostrich

When it comes to
challenges in your life or in
your career, burying your
head in the sand is never a
good idea.

When I think of an ostrich, I am reminded of the images of the large, unwieldy bird with his head buried in the sand. In these images, there is generally some danger lurking in the background, ready to befall the ostrich as he blissfully remains ignorant.

There are many ostrich bosses, particularly those in middle-management positions that simply choose ignorance over information. These ostrich bosses don't want to know what they don't know.

This ignorance is generally the precursor to blaming poor communication or other people for their lack of performance.

I recently quit a position at a mental health clinic as an Administrative Supervisor. This position was a few steps down for me, but because of the ailing economy I took the position. My boss was the Clinic Manager, a social worker who had been promoted to this position two years earlier.

The position I took was held by a person who had worked her way up to the position and was retiring after 22 years. Her retirement was put on hold so that she could train the new hire. Unfortunately, the person who previously held the position was upset because her retirement had been delayed so that she could train the new person (me), but then she refused to train me. My supervisor told me she was only to show me where things were.

Over the five months there, I received no training from the previous person, no formal training in the different programs I was responsible for: payroll, purchasing, safety, etc. It turned out that although my supervisor had been there two years, she knew very little about my job.

I used my previous work experience in HR, and my degree in business with a minor in technology to help me figure out the different computer programs and was able to keep everyone paid and the office supplied; however, the process (state civil service) was incredibly frustrating.

My attempts to get the training I needed were unsuccessful. My attempts to get help from my supervisor were also unsuccessful. She would respond to my requests for help with a directive to keep her informed of when I would have the training I needed.

All contact with her involved her loading me up with more work than I was possibly able to do. She spoke to me and the other supervisors like we were children, and any questions asked were answered with a long explanation of why the question was stupid or why your idea would never work. It never mattered whether she was right or wrong or even understood the question. Her tactics were to micromanage and bully all of the workers.

I was also required to manage and supervise three workers in a satellite clinic. When I explained that I had no time to do this I was told to carve out the time just like she did. When I explained that I had a full work load (unlike the other supervisors who had a much lessened work load and no employees to supervise at the other location), I was told that everyone had the same work load.

I finally realized that my department had two frozen positions, one above my position and one at the lowest level, and that I was performing these duties. I also finally realized that the previous employee in my position was not doing the duties I was responsible for.

She never went to the other clinic. She never had to do the work of all absent (disgruntled) employees, and she was also allowed to work and receive time and one-half leave for working overtime.

In this position I experienced: discrimination, bullying, micromanagement, and harassment. The worst boss ever!

The frustration and confusion from this previous story and that faced by countless people in the workplace does not come from open intentional hostility. Instead, it comes from ostrich bosses who choose not to communicate and would prefer to bury their heads in the sand instead of dealing with the challenges of the situation.

Ostrich bosses spend an inordinate amount of time making sure you understand their feelings while they spend very little effort and energy trying to understand your point of view.

Ostrich bosses have never discovered that the Golden Rule applies to the workplace.

How about a boss who, after 13 years of being your employer, doesn't talk to you, look at you, otherwise acknowledge you? You work full time and have to beg for annual reviews and raises. You are supposed to get a cash bonus twice per month, and the boss is always late to give it, or simply thinks he already did, so you get cheated. No appreciation for his staff—especially the long-term, hard-working employees. After two weeks of earned pay, they hand you the paycheck and ask you to wait a few days to cash or deposit the check! Poor ventilation and cooling in the building where the grunts work. They couldn't care less. Their offices have AC!

A non-responsive, non-communicative ostrich boss does not only affect the people immediately around them, but, over time, they begin to represent the whole organization.

This is a tribute to not only a horrible boss, but a horrible company. I don't even know who my boss is.

My actual supervisor resigned about a year ago, and they did not rehire the position. After a few months when they re-did the organizational chart and realized I didn't report to anyone, they (whoever "they" are) placed me under the VP—whose role changed about a month later—and I just kept waiting for someone to come explain the change and tell me who I should report to.

Nothing. Not a word. It's been about eight months, and I still don't know who I report to. Even though I don't get many company updates, I have survived about six rounds of layoffs, and I get to come and go as I please.

Good people in the workplace can disagree and even argue at times. This is preferable to being ignored entirely.

In a sales job that I had previously, my Sales Manager had a bad habit of not clearly communicating his expectations for our sales activity. After one particularly confusing email, I replied to the message and asked for clarification.

Later that day, he called me and the rest of our sales team (two other people) into his office and proceeded to chew me out in front of my peers about questioning his expectations. I tried to clarify that I just wanted to be sure I knew what I was going to be held accountable for, but he was so angry that my attempts were in vain.

One of my teammates quit the next day and later that day my manager and his manager asked me to decide if I wanted to continue working there. Um....no thanks.

Moral: Turns out my manager was under a lot of pressure from his manager and the branch manager to bring his team's numbers up. Doesn't justify it, but I learned that there's usually more to the story than we know about.

An ostrich boss with their head buried firmly in the sand will become hostile if you force them to stand up and look at the reality of the situation. This hostility will be directed at you, even if you are alerting them to a real and imminent danger.

Almost any approach is preferable to doing nothing. If you are in a position where you are forced to deal with an ostrich boss, you will have to document all your actions and create what I call the "non-response response." This comes in the form of documented correspondence that you keep on file stating, "Dear Ostrich Boss: We are faced with the following situation... Based on this, I believe we should take this action I am outlining... We need to move on this by the end of the month for this strategy to be effective. Please let me know your thoughts. Otherwise, I will simply proceed as outlined above."

An ostrich boss is worse than no boss at all. At least when you determine you are dealing with an ostrich boss, you can start to take charge of the situation, document your actions, and move ahead. If your ostrich boss is the only one in the organization with their head buried in the sand, they will be discovered and removed quickly, particularly if you document your actions through the "non-response response."

If you are dealing with an entire organization of ostriches, you need to update your resume, alert your network of contacts, and prepare to move.

If you are flying on an airplane being piloted by someone whose head is buried in the sand, it is only a matter of time until you and everyone involved meet with disaster.

CHAPTER SIX

The Snapping Turtle

Mature human beings
exhibit a range of feelings
and emotions. Immature
ones only ignore or snap.

As young children, many of us—at least for a short period of time—had a pet turtle. The name "turtle" has come to define a number of different creatures that have widely varying characteristics.

Most of us who had pet turtles actually had a terrapin. These are extremely docile creatures that rarely, if ever, harm anyone. There are a number of similar species that are prevalent, depending on where you might live. Then, finally, there is the dreaded snapping turtle.

A snapping turtle may look like a terrapin and act very docile, just as the terrapin does. One is likely to discover they are dealing with a snapping turtle instead of a terrapin very suddenly and quite violently. Snapping turtles will react to any situation by remaining totally motionless in their shell or by viciously snapping at anything in front of them.

Snapping turtle bosses act similarly; however, they are less predictable than the four-legged variety. The thing that causes a snapping turtle boss to snap at you may or may not have anything to do with you specifically. This makes snapping turtle bosses very unpredictable and very dangerous.

A woman in Alabama, re-entering the workforce, found this out the hard way.

For 13 years, I was a stay-at-home mother and wife. Unfortunately, the marriage did not work out and in order to survive, I had to find a job.

My first job was with a large Fortune 500 Company. I started out in the copy room (reproduction). My job was making copies of documents. I ran these machines all day long. There were two of them.

I was afraid of my boss. I think she really enjoyed intimidating everyone that worked for her. It was like walking on eggshells every day. It was such an unpleasant environment.

The one thing that stands out in my mind is the day that she walked into the copy room, picked up a stapler, and tried to staple a document she had in her hand. There were no staples in the stapler.

She looked at me and with those big blazing red eyes said, "Do you know what I tend to do when I want to use a stapler that has no staples?"

I said "No Ma'am, I do not know."

She said, "I throw the stapler."

And that is exactly what she did. She threw the stapler over my head and hit the wall behind me.

It was a very difficult time for me. I had gone through a divorce and had three sons to raise. My father had just passed away, and my life was already very emotional and stressful. But she was the icing on the cake.

The other employee that worked with me (not in the copy room but in the administrative room) told me that I should report her to HR. I did not, because I was afraid of losing my job; but someone did because in about two weeks she was transferred to another location.

What a sigh of relief to get rid of her!!! Not only for me but all the others that she made so miserable.

Often, the behavior of a snapping turtle boss is so outrageous under the specific circumstances that it is difficult to deal with the situation if no one else observes the behavior. Other times, everyone knows about the snapping turtle boss, but the group chooses to ignore the behavior out of fear and intimidation.

A very long time ago—and in a very different life—I had the misfortune to accept a job with a law firm in my little town. The position was secretarial and though I had no formal training as such, I was able to maneuver around legal terminology without falling into mind-numbing perplexity.

My day consisted of finding 7 to 10 tapes on my desk every morning with no instruction other than what was on the tapes, determining which files the tapes related to, pulling and reviewing, then transcribing what was dictated. The end result—either correspondence or motions for filing—were to be delivered late the same day unto my liege for his review. If success had been achieved in translating what he conveyed on the tapes, signatures occurred and mailing or filing with the courts ensued. Fairly straightforward stuff.

On a particular day, one tape in the bundle was left with unclear instruction. My lord liege was away on a few days R&R. I completed the task as directed; however, as I had training and experience as a law clerk, I took the file to the next level and completed what was required to expedite the matter. Due to his vacation, timing on the file was grossly shortened, which would have been disastrous for the paying client.

Upon my superior's return, he discovered what had transpired (under the auspices and direction to me from a Senior Lawyer) and began to berate me—in front of all the other secretaries.

Now, being a fairly tough-skinned and -minded kinda gal, it was no huge harassment deal for me. It was only when he shouted out—very loud—"You don't need to think. You only have to do this!" And he held out his hands and mimicked typing with his fingers.

I laughed out loud, picked up my gear and told him that he was now free to do it for himself as it was impossible for me not to think. He was a pompous, self-righteous, self-centered, and smelly guy (he always ate truly inappropriate *foods at the office that gave him disgusting gas that he passed freely and frequently).*

I felt better leaving that employment and moving on to a much more fulfilling career.

On the up-side of the experience, I now understand all those lawyer jokes.

Snapping turtle bosses can snap for random reasons that have nothing to do with what they are snapping at, or they may snap because you have inadvertently violated an unwritten, previously unknown rule that only exists in the snapping turtle boss's brain.

I was a fresh young college graduate and very excited about starting my first job. I worked in the Personnel Department as the suggestion manager for a large manufacturing facility. The basic duties of this job was to take the suggestions from the workforce and process them to see if they could be instituted and if they saved the company any money to give out cash awards to the employee.

One day I handed out a report on a suggestion to a group headed by the plant manager. During our conversation, the plant manager seemed to be having difficulty finding something in my report, so I walked around to his side of the desk to help him find it.

At that point he blew up! He cussed and yelled at me for walking around to his side of the desk. He stated it was disrespectful and continued to question my ancestry and brains with the top of his voice. The other four people in the room just looked at their shoes. I was stunned.

After the meeting, the others came around and tried to reassure me that I had done nothing wrong. The next day the plant manager stopped me in the hall, when no one was around, and apologized. He yelled in public and apologized in private.

I will always remember his name and use this example when teaching what not to do as a supervisor.

To this day, if I saw a bus bearing down on him, and had the time to pull him out of the way...well...it would be a tough decision.

A woman in Virginia discovered that a snapping turtle boss can bite clear across the Atlantic Ocean.

My boss is from England. He is 5'3 and throws temper tantrums that would make Mommy Dearest seem like an angel. He jumps up and down, gets red in the face, and throws things at walls in hopes that someone will step in front of his missile. He disregards all laws and refuses to comply with anything outside of his personal wishes.

Salaried employees are docked pay on a regular basis. All 35 employees are afraid for their jobs, and in this economy new jobs are not easy to find. Then he has the audacity to lie about his behavior to the owners of the company.

Beside the word Tyrant in the dictionary is my boss's photograph.

When I was around five or six years old, visiting my grandparents, I found a turtle in the yard and asked my grandfather if I could keep it. He said yes, but knowing it was a snapping turtle, he offered me a brief demonstration.

He took out a pencil and poked it near the turtle's head. The turtle instantly extended its neck and snapped off the end of the pencil.

My grandfather allowed the experience to sink in a moment and then asked, "Now that you've seen what he can do, if he bites off your finger, is it his fault or yours?"

When dealing with a snapping turtle boss, you've got to determine if you're willing and able to deal with the periodic snaps. Over time, you can learn to diffuse them and stay out of the way, but in the short term, you have to realize it is the nature of the beast.

CHAPTER SEVEN

The Hyena

Sticks and stones may
break my bones, but words
can cut into my heart and
soul.

Hyenas are known for their distinctive voice. It has been described as laughing, barking, or braying, but whatever you call it, if you've ever heard a hyena, you will never forget it.

If you've ever had the misfortune of being in a verbal confrontation that ended up as a physical altercation, it's likely that your memories of the event revolve around the words spoken to you in anger, not the pain and physical injuries you might have received. Words become memories that are indelibly etched in our hearts and on our minds.

Hyena bosses are those careless or even vicious individuals who use their tongue as a weapon. Unfortunately, most employees don't feel the freedom to defend themselves verbally when they are attacked by a hyena boss. These thoughtless and painful words emanating from a hyena boss can remain with you for many years.

When I was in high school, I worked in a locally owned clothing store. The owner was not known for giving words of encouragement to his employees.

One Saturday I made a sale to a lady and her young son. After making the sale, the owner came to me and asked what I had sold them. I told him: a suit, shirt, tie, belt, socks and shoes.

He looked at me and asked, "Did you sell them any underwear?"

I told him, "No."

He just looked down and walked away, shaking his head. Seems nothing was good enough for him.

Some hyena bosses have a wide repertoire of verbal arrows they can shoot. Their comments can range from vague and unclear to painful, vicious, and destructive.

In 2007, I accepted an HR job at a local steel company after 3 months of recruiting efforts on their part. At first, I thought my new boss would be cool as we liked the same type of music, food, etc.

Once hired, I was given very little to do. He told me that he was hoping for a cat fight between me and the HR Manager, suggesting that I needed to forcefully gain more responsibility.

Then, he told me that since I wasn't a morning person, I could come in and work fluctuating hours...8-5, 9-6. I told him that I would stay at 8-5. He then said that he *needed me in at 7:30, so I started coming in at 7:30. Well, that didn't work, and he told me that he didn't mean that I had to come in at that time EVERY day, so I would vary from 7:30-4:30 or 8-5. At that point, he said that I needed to be there at 7:30 everyday.*

Shortly after my hire, the battery in my SUV died. A couple of days later he invited me to lunch (at my fav restaurant, no less) to tell me that he was concerned about my performance. He said that he was disappointed that I missed 1.5 hours due to my car issues, and that if I had totally replaced all of the parts on my SUV that could possibly stop working, that I would not have had this trouble and that I obviously didn't think ahead. Who on earth replaces every part on their car when they get a new job?

At that point, he kept on me about my religious preference. A month later, I was let go. The woman that I had replaced came back to work there, even though he had nothing positive to say about her while I was there. The reason for my lay-off was lack of work; so why do you hire a replacement for me in 3 days?

It has been 1.5 years since I worked there, and my hands are shaking as I write this.

Oh, he was always telling me that he was personally chosen by God to suffer all of the idiots that he had to deal with as an HR Director (he was always quoting the bible). BUT, he has slept with several women at the plant, told me to take a litter of kittens out back and slam their heads against the cement...Mr. Religious! Also, every time he would fire someone, he would be super-excited, do a little jig and say, "I'm gonna fire their ass!" What a jerk,

I am so glad that I no longer work there.

My mom and I attended a concert shortly after my termination and he crossed the road in front of my car. My mom (age 73) told me to run over the SOB. It was hilarious. I didn't run over him, but he did give me a funny look. That was the last that I ever saw of him.

Among all the worst bosses stories I have received, some of the most outrageous fall into the hyena boss category. I have written a number of novels and consider myself a good writer of dialogue; however, if I had written some of the lines uttered by hyena bosses, the publishers and readers of my books would have laughed out loud at the unbelievable words attributed to hyena bosses.

A Canadian woman found this out the hard way.

I had a job while I was in university at a very prestigious department store chain. I worked for a skin care line in the cosmetics department.

I've always been into fashion and make up, and I loved the organization, loved the product, loved my customers. I also earned very decent money as a part time commissioned sales rep. although my paycheques often went back into the store to buy clothes, shoes, jewelry, or cosmetics.

The only thing I didn't like about this job was the crazy scary manager that ran the cosmetics department. This department as a whole did very well compared to other cities in terms of sales. I believe it's in spite of the fact that the manager instilled such fear in the staff, they were afraid of what would happen if they didn't reach their sales quota each week.

So, I was a 19 year old psych student, working part time at this job to support my shopping habit. At the time my father also owned and operated a chain of retail stores (sports and outerwear product) and I also worked in one of his stores on the other side of the city, part time whenever I could. Needless to say, I grew up working in the 're-tail world' and pretty much breathed customer service! (I think I started working when I was 9!!)

One day at the large department store, I was helping a customer to select a skin care product, and I was asked a question I couldn't answer about one of the ingredients in the product. I told the lady that I wasn't sure on the answer to her question, but certainly could find out for her. I would just have to look it up in our product manual. She told me that it was okay, it wasn't that important, and would buy it anyway. So I sold her the product.

CHAPTER EIGHT

The Looney Bird

Some people are so crazy
that, merely by being
associated with them, you
have a hard time retaining
your own sanity.

Looney birds are among nature's most bizarre and offbeat characters. In the workplace, looney bird bosses create a surreal environment around them that can make everyone crazy. The dangerous part of having a looney bird boss is that, over time, even the most absurd environment can begin to seem normal. At that point, the looney bird boss is not only acting crazy but begins to draw everyone else into the behavior.

A gentleman in England got caught up in a looney bird boss's nest.

This was an eco construction company which had the right ingredients to establish itself as a forerunner in the construction industry.

The unfortunate thing about this "boss" was that they have great vision but little understanding of managing a team. There were no boundaries at work, and the company revolved closely around the boss and her personal life.

When I initially went for an informal interview, the boss had a gentleman sitting alongside her, who was presented as her business partner. After showing some of my design work and discussing what I could bring to the company, it was agreed that I would fit in well and bring some very useful capabilities. Then after many phone calls to try and establish my start date, my first day at work encountered one business partner (and boyfriend) gone and another in his place (business partner and boyfriend that is).

I should have followed my instinct and left at this point, but the feeling of opportunity and of not having witnessed anything personally kept me in my seat; however, people (clients, employees, and a previous boyfriend) seemed to have various problems with this boss, and atmospheres at work were beginning to become strange.

In an attempt to not become involved I took the head down (headphones on, music up) approach to my working day. The boss justified this seemingly odd response people were having towards her as a reaction (from largely builders) towards a powerful, successful woman. And the problem with clients and contractors was to due to the economic downturn, etc. Both seemed plausible but not entirely believable.

My work was getting praise, and money came at the end of each week, but more and more employees were deciding to "jump ship and swim for shore". The workforce began to dwindle (some of their own accord, some by dismissal from the boss). Communication with clients began to seize up, the current business partner/boyfriend left and things seemed in tatters; however, I remained to support my employer in what is now an economic recession around the globe.

Unfortunately the closer I got, the more visible the truth became, and I began to experience some of the behavior that had made others flee for their sanity.

After these experiences and research towards the strange and distressing experience I was having, I discovered the "boss" in question has a symptom called narcissistic personality disorder—one which enables them to strive for success and admiration but not able to empathize with her team to develop any kind of true cohesion in the company, and at its worst, display some completely dismissive negative reactions towards work produced by others and offer little or no support to help rectify the apparent mess they were creating—thus, unfortunately, leaving people that encounter their behavior (that of the boss with NPD) feeling confused, useless, and unable to understand where it all went wrong.

As someone who studied psychology in depth as part of my university degree program, I can assure you that giving a looney bird boss's behavior a formal diagnoses such as narcissistic personality disorder may make you feel better, but it won't change the behavior or work environment.

A looney bird boss by any other name still creates insanity.

I worked in an independent bookstore where the owner was very forgetful.

One day she'd say, "I want you to fill this table full of books from independent publishers, and make it as full as you can." The next day she'd come by and say, "I want you to only have one or two copies of each of those books on that table." On the third day, she'd call you in and demand to know why that table wasn't stuffed full like she'd told you to do it.

We finally took to writing down everything she told us to do so we could show her what she had said.

She was also very cheap. One time I noticed a bunch of used books with odd prices—$2.61, $4.58, etc. It seems the number 9 had worn off the pricing gun from overuse and she was too cheap to buy another one.

Looney bird bosses may be forgetful, delusional, or crazy. Unfortunately, they set the boundaries and provide the environment in the workplace. The looney bird boss's perception will inevitably become your reality.

One of my worst bosses was a very young lady who had married the boss. He was a laid-back guy, but she was wound pretty tight. He stepped away from the company and left her in charge and it was a nightmare from hell.

Everything about her, from her skintight leopard print pants to her enormously high heels to her fake tan and nails, screamed DRAMA.

She burst into tears in a conference once after accusing all the managers of not caring about the company as much as he and she did and only coming to work to get a paycheck. Well, duh.

Once, in a marketing meeting, to show us how good the product supposedly was, she ate a dog biscuit. We all just stared at her with our mouths open. I guess she was right about us not caring for the company as much as she did.

Newsflash: No matter how much you pay me, I'm never going to eat dog food.

There are very few absolutes in human interaction and organizational dynamics; however, even given the example of a looney bird boss, eating pet food should always be considered out of bounds!

Then there are cases in which a looney bird boss's influence becomes so pervasive it turns into looney bird policies.

My worst boss hired me, and set me up with a supervisor who was a great individual contributor, but a lousy mentor.

I was hired to use a computer, but due to regulations and politics, I could not get a password until I attended three consecutive classes. When I asked when I could get in the classes, they did not know. It turns out that I would wait 5 months to attend all the classes in the proper sequence and get the required password. My boss and supervisor claimed I was lazy for those 5 months, when they did not give me the training or password needed to use the computer for the job I was hired to do.

During the first 5 months, I would ask the mentor a question, and he'd frequently respond with a gentle verbal abuse such as, "Like I told you last week..." or "We went over this before..." I began taking notes of my conversations with him and learned he never did make the comments he claimed. He made it where I dreaded asking him a question. Questions were not opportunities for him to help out a co-worker, rather, they were opportunities for him to harass employees.

When they finally got me into the training class required for me to get my passwords, I was told I would have to drive other coworkers to the remote city for the same training. I thought I would travel during the day. Instead, I was informed by my boss that I would have to work all day at the office, then pick up the coworkers in a company vehicle, and drive them on my personal time to the remote city. The next day, I was to attend the all day class, drive the coworkers back on personal time, and I was to also wash & clean the car before it was dropped off.

During a heavy workload, there was a call for mandatory overtime and weekend work. After I finally got my password, I was ordered to come in on a Saturday. When I arrived, my PC was unusable to me because it was under several weekend software upgrades by the IT department. I was told I had to be at my desk, even though the PC was unusable due to the software upgrades going on by IT. With nothing to do, since I required a computer to do my job, I cleaned my desk. I was reprimanded by my boss for cleaning my desk, even though my computer was unusable on a mandatory Saturday workday, with nothing to do.

One of my favorite authors and mentors often warns that "We become like the people we hang around with all day." This is important to remember when dealing with a looney bird boss.

If you're only dealing with one individual, you may be able to document the behavior and be the instigator for change; however, if the looney bird behavior has affected the entire organization, you may be forced to move on or risk your own sanity.

CHAPTER NINE

The Fox

Some people inadvertently harm you. Others do it because it's simply their nature. But the most dangerous people actually scheme against you.

In literature and lore, the fox is thought to be scheming and conniving. The old phrase "having the fox guard the henhouse" is indicative of someone in a position of responsibility who is irresponsible and untrustworthy.

Fox bosses are dangerous, not only to subordinates but to upper management and the entire organization as well.

It was that time again. The end of the third quarter had passed, and it was time to report the company's earnings to the public.

Amidst all the new requirements for Sarbanes-Oxley, the corporate accounting team was working diligently to meet the difficult deadlines typically experienced every quarter and year-end.

Financial reporting and analysis can be quite difficult at a Fortune 500 company given the data to report is spread across many countries and continents. My role, similar to others on the team was to complete my assigned footnotes and assist with the aggregation of financial statement data. I had been doing this now for about 6 or 7 quarters so I was very familiar with the challenges and bottlenecks standing in my way.

I can remember working long hours and Saturdays with a new baby at home. I often wondered when I was going to figure out what I really wanted to do for a living.

Eric (we'll call him this as it is not his real name) was particularly difficult to work with. As the head of the department he would often talk about himself at the weekly staff meetings and appeared as though he was often uncomfortable in his own skin.

I recall a staff meeting where the team had been casually talking prior to the start, as we usually did, about events going on in the world. We enjoyed each others' company and tried to make the most of working the long hours away from our families. Eric typically let the air out of our sails by making a joke that was insulting sometimes to women or minorities or talking about himself.

One of the team members made a small joke about Eric in the meeting which was a response to a comment Eric made in jest. The team member's joke was harmless and in no way offensive. Eric quickly lost his cool and told everyone to report back to their desk as the meeting was over. He made it very clear he was the only one allowed to make a joke at a meeting.

The department was mostly women, and they often took offense at his smug comments which typically implied that women were not built for the big corporate world. Eric would typically ask most of the young women in the department the occasional question of when they planned to have their first or second child. He often pried into the personal lives of the staff as a way to make conversation and provide his opinion on various subjects such as parenting and home repair.

When we weren't closing the books for the quarter we were often reviewing budget line items and working on the following year's budget. I recall finding a line item which was double-counted in the overall budget. This was a significant dollar amount and a real win for the department since now costs would be much less for the year than originally budgeted. I was proud to have uncovered the issue and reluctantly reported the good news to Eric. He wasn't too thrilled with the find, and I determined his motives rather quickly as I sat in his office. The CFO walked into his office as I sat there and interrupted our conversation which he had the obvious authority to do.

He is a very pleasant person and said hello to both of us. He appeared to be quite happy and asked Eric who was responsible for the discovery of a savings related to the budget. Eric didn't pause or hesitate and didn't look at me. He quickly replied, "Well, it was me." The CFO said, "Great job," and walked to his office.

I was quite upset especially considering Eric didn't even discuss his blatant lie with me as I sat in his office for the next few minutes. He continued our previous *conversation as though the CFO never stopped in for a chat. He really believed he was the hero of the day simply because he was in charge.*

Fox bosses that steal the praise and accolades that their team deserves damage not only the employees who are deprived of the recognition they have earned, but the fox boss actually diminishes himself as he can no longer take credit for assembling and managing a great team.

I work at a huge discount retail store. ONE of my MANY managers is always stealing credit for other people's work; but at the same time if he makes a merchandising decision, and the store manager doesn't like the feature, this manager will blame it on the associate saying it was his/her idea.

Once an associate thought she was having a mild stroke. The left side of her body went numb, and she asked if she could go to the hospital. The manager said, "No, you'll be getting help soon enough." So she stayed to work for some unbelievable reason.

A fox boss who will take credit for something he didn't do while blaming team members for his own failings is more than enough to deal with, without being denied medical attention while having a stroke.

Truth is stranger than fiction.

I worked for a large utility company in their environmental compliance group under a horrible manager from about 1980 through 1991. He was a married man who was covertly (or so he thought) having an affair with one of my coworkers who was also married, but not to him.

Every year, our company required that each of its employees be given a performance review. My job was as an environmental specialist responsible for hazardous waste disposal and the PCB situation in the company which at that time was a hot topic.

I had worked particularly hard that year, often being called out to work PCB spills in the middle of the night and on weekends. During my performance review, my manager told me that I didn't know anything about the law and generally degraded my work and me personally. I determined right then and there that I would learn something about the law and would never again work for a jerk like him or a company that allowed its employees to be supervised by a person such as him who didn't have the slightest idea about how to manage people and didn't understand that the number one reason that people leave their jobs is that they do not feel appreciated.

I maintained my job there while I attended law school at night, with the company paying all of the cost for my schooling. When I obtained my law degree, I quit my job and began my law career. I am now successfully operating my own law firm where I try to apply the lessons that I learned from my former boss about how not to treat employees.

The only way you can outfox a fox boss is to succeed while they are trying to make you fail.

A woman in Australia experienced the total destruction that a scheming fox boss can create.

I worked for a clothes manufacturer and retailer in the 1980s. Our company was bought out, and the new firm gave our beloved manager the boot, paid him out, and replaced him with a manager who was notorious for running companies into the ground. Of course, he kept butting heads with us in the management team because we were dedicated to the company (and the 40+ stores across Australia) to make sure we stayed the market leader.

The new boss was a sleaze bucket to say the least. He had affair after affair with staff from previous companies and had a fling with one of the store managers to whom he showed tremendous favor. He had absolute foul breath and smelt awfully of smoke, etc., and never looked groomed. He was always looking at you up and down, and you felt he was mentally undressing you. Really creepy stuff.

He set out to make all staff redundant by closing the manufacturing arm and buying in cheap tee shirts, jeans, etc., from China which was absolute rubbish. Not good quality at all, and he got one or two of the factory workers to stay and sew our company labels into all the rubbish he imported.

We knew the writing was on the wall for all of us that wouldn't do things the way he wanted to because we were all likeminded and honest, hard working people, and one by one he set about ear marking us for the boot.

He took a really wonderful company and ran it into the ground. A lot of sweet factory workers lost their jobs which was very sad for them—they were all committed to doing really good work. For us in administration, we all went on to other companies and have maintained successful careers, but I often wonder about the factory staff who were so disadvantaged and treated so poorly by this horrible boss.

Well, enough said. That is my horror story. Much more to be said, but not in words that are printable.

Some bosses are well-meaning but incompetent. Their best efforts often lead to failure. But fox bosses have motives that do not serve their subordinates, upper management, or the organization as a whole.

Fox bosses should be dealt with like an armed thief. They are trying to take what is not theirs while threatening everyone around them.

If you are dealing with a fox boss, you owe it to the entire organization and to yourself to document the atrocities, and take it to top management or ownership. You may lose your position, but if no one will listen to you and heed your warning, it's only a matter of time until the entire organization crashes and burns anyway.

CHAPTER TEN

The Mole

Someone can be out of
sight and even out of mind,
but it doesn't mean they're
beyond hurting you and
destroying the entire
organization.

Moles are thought of as being cute little furry creatures that are harmless. This is until they tunnel under your yard or a golf course. Then they become an insidious menace, destroying everything in their path.

Mole bosses proceed as if no one can observe their underground behavior, and they are often oblivious to everything else going on in the organization above ground and in the light of day.

After I was hired as a divisional HR Manager, I was introduced to the VP, Administration— the man to whom I had a heavily dotted reporting line. During this meeting, he told me that he really did not have any respect for HR and that the company could easily get along without any of the HR team, with the exception of one person in the department. I later realized that he liked her, not necessarily for her professional talent, but more for her good looks. This guy truly was the embodiment of the dirty old man.

About 18 months later, after I had been laid off and his wife had died, I learned that he'd had an affair with the receptionist who had recently left her husband! The age difference was about 25 to 30 years. His behaviour was not exactly a shining example of how a senior executive should behave toward a subordinate.

A few months after I had joined, we were in the midst of a North American turndown in our business. We were at one of our weekly management meetings and the sales manager had just given us a detailed report on how bleak sales were despite the sales team's best efforts.

My boss then replied, "I don't know what's wrong out there, but you had better change these numbers really soon!"

It was as if he had not paid any attention at all to the presentation, and he certainly did not have anything positive to share with us. All of us thought that he did not really understand the market conditions, he did he know anything about sales—which was true—and he did not offer any advice or assistance to the sales manager.

None of us had any respect for this man and often regarded him as a fine example of incompetence.

This mole boss assumed his undercover activities were a secret while he remained unaware of the day-to-day operations in the company and overall trends in the economy. This is a very dangerous combination.

My worst boss was actually a conglomeration of administrators to whom I reported. The three men combined to form the perfect yes-man. They would do whatever their superiors wanted without any regard for what was in the best interest of their direct reports or the programs they were responsible for supervising. They were great PR guys who possessed little substance or fortitude to support and go to bat for me or other mid-level managers who the administration knew were doing the job we had been hired to do.

Even though we were making great strides toward improving the effectiveness and compliance of the programs and holding our staff members accountable for their time and expenses, the administrators chose to throw us under the bus to avoid taking the time to respond to a witch hunt that had been instigated by former (and current) staff members who had taken advantage of the system for decades.

This mole boss team was working under the surface to undermine the dedicated people really doing the work. Unfortunately, by the time you discover the sub-surface damage created by mole bosses, the organizational patient may be terminal.

Some mole bosses attempt to hide the truth underground, even during the hiring process. By the time this activity is discovered, it can be too late.

I had been offered a job that was an OUTSIDE sales position for a computer education/training facility. The job description had said I would be working in the field, visiting businesses, and promoting/marketing the company.

Before I even met most people in the office, they put me on a plane to San Antonio, TX for a two-week training session, with all expenses paid. I had never worked for a company who did this before.

Once I got back, the job description became a bait-and-switch. I was not working in the field. I was working in a telemarketing position in a boiler-room atmosphere. I was not even furnished with qualified leads. I had to work the local phone book in a dialing-for-dollars job.

There were quotas for many aspects of the job: number of calls per hour, amount of time on the phone, number of set appointments and/or introductory classes, etc., and they got down on us if we fell short on any quotas.

The worst part of the job was the last-minute Lunch & Learns which were usually announced within one hour of our lunch. Instead of being able to go anywhere and do whatever we wanted on our lunch break, we had 5 or 10 minutes to grab or purchase our lunch in the building's cafeteria and sit in the adjoining meeting room and be forced to sit through our unpaid lunch to listen to a variety of BS presenters or topics.

After 90 days, I was fired (thank goodness) because I didn't meet all my quotas (even though this was not my original job description). Not too long after that came 9/11, and from what I learned from some people who I knew there, despite the news of the attacks, management required them to continue making calls. I bet they had a mandatory Lunch & Learn that day as well.

I never would have thought that a company that was that generous at the beginning was so slave-driving and disrespectful to their employees once training was over. I'm not sure if they are still in business, but they deserve to go under!

Mole bosses thrive underground and believe they will succeed if they keep you in the dark as long as possible.

So my story is a little different then some, or maybe not depending on what you have seen.

This was very early in my working days. My boss, other than loving to make his employee's cry with his angry and hostile attitude, was also having an affair with one of the girls under him.

Well, the unfortunate thing was that I did not happen to like this co-worker. While I was never out right rude or mean to her, I didn't really associate with her unless needed. Well, the co-worker was a bit on the sensitive side and decided to complain to boyfriend AKA the boss about this. When my review came up a couple of weeks later, I was not surprised to see that I was marked down on it because of my lack of team work and my rude demeanor to other co-workers.

Since I was working for a company that did not have an HR department and my boss was also the owner, I did not have a lot of resources available to me. After leaving the company I found out through a friend that was still working there that the boss's wife discovered the affair, divorced the boss, and took his company in the divorce. Karma I guess.

Mole bosses often get what they deserve, but many times it's too late. Their covert efforts can take everyone down the tubes. Mole bosses not only work to keep you in the dark, but they elicit others in their game so that the deception can multiply.

I've worked in the HR field for almost a decade, and in order to get out of Las Vegas and back to small town living, I took a title and pay cut to move to a small town.

No longer a manager, I came across an HR manager that has absolutely no ethics or morals. Not only has he asked me out countless times, but when I refused, I got the silent treatment! He's smart enough not to retaliate, but the silent treatment? Come on. I haven't done that since elementary school!

And what's worse, now the comments made in my presence, and to many other females in the company, are perverse and inappropriate. Jokes are off color, and innuendoes about his personal life are unacceptable. I've voiced my opinion to him; and he now knows when he's off-color and I'm around, he better get back on track quickly, because I'm not one of the ignorant small town girls that will take it!

Mole bosses thrive while underground and in the dark. Your best defense for a mole boss is to simply expose them to the light of day.

The best mole boss antidote is to begin the relationship with specific and pointed questions. Then follow up with confirmation in writing. "I'm very pleased to be accepting a position with a company that guarantees.... I'm grateful for your assurances...."

The mole boss will flee from the light of their own actions and the confinement of your specific questions.

CHAPTER ELEVEN

The Snake

People will continue to
frustrate us as long as we
expect them to act contrary
to their nature.

Snakes have been blamed for every conflict and ill deed since the Garden of Eden. They are often deadly and always frightening. Snakes create the image of a hidden, lurking serpent, ready to strike without warning.

Snake bosses come in all shapes and sizes. Some of them are, indeed, deadly while others are simply a constant menace.

The worst boss I ever had was a manipulative, impulsive, lazy, dishonest egotist who treated our office like her non-stop Sweet 16 party.

At first, I thought she was merely strange and perhaps in over her head in our department. She painted one of our offices with spray paint, adding peace signs and messages like Keep the Faith but, when a new company president expressed distaste for the paint job, she lied that maintenance had thought of the idea. It was then I realized she was not kooky but harmful.

She kept morale low by swearing, screaming, and loudly threatening to get other managers, even her superiors, fired. Perhaps suspecting her own incompetence, she acted frequently out of paranoia, fearing that everyone was out to get her.

She terminated one of her employees after seeing her engaged in a friendly chat with the company president. She would cry when she was under fire, if she couldn't blame someone else, and frequently responded to criticism from management by calling her lawyer.

While we worked, she would put her feet up and brag about her sex life. She asked impertinent, unprofessional questions. She was a walking lawsuit. She said offensive things and cursed to colleagues and vendors. She always called an older black female employee Mama and would talk to her in Ebonics, even though she, herself, was a white woman from rural Illinois.

She had no work ethic or professionalism. Her favorite expressions were "Cover your ass" and "Not my problem." When our fax machine malfunctioned when I had a large fax to send, she told me to "Have fun."

Our office had constant deadlines, but she ignored them. Once, she was more interested in throwing an orange from hand to hand instead of reviewing a piece with a deadline only hours away. Still, she demanded to oversee everything I did, even though doing so devastated our productivity.

Most likely I wager this was so that she could take credit for our good ideas.

She stole notes I had prepared for a meeting with our vice president and had attempted to start quoting my ideas as if they were hers. Fortunately, I suspected this and spoke up before she could. After the meeting, she loudly called me a backstabbing bitch on a phone call.

Her favoritism was rampant and overt.

Snake bosses have a tendency to either lie dormant or strike viciously. It's hard to find any middle ground and impossible to know what triggers them.

One of our computer techs was struggling with some issues and had to go on medical leave. Everyone was concerned about him because he was a smoker and had health issues. He was very talented and knowledgeable about computers. We all relied on him for information and for fixing laptops.

One day, almost 30 days into his leave, my boss announced in the office very loudly during a phone call with someone else that he was on the psych ward at the local hospital wearing a white jacket and that she really missed him and his talent. My jaw just fell.

The next week she was interviewing job replacements for him on the phone. Soon after, she announced very loudly on the phone that she had talked to him recently and that he was under the misguided impression that he had a job waiting for him when he got back.

Snake bosses do not have the willingness or the ability to empathize with the circumstances or challenges that others may be facing. Snake bosses only register things in their environment as they perceive it might affect them.

A Canadian woman found this out the hard way.

My boss was the CEO. A fellow worker's husband dies, and the boss would not allow any of us to have any contact with her. We were told not to call her. The boss said she was a very private person! When the funeral came, none of us were allowed to go as she did not want any work missed!

When our colleague came back, our boss hauled us all into the board room and told us we were not to talk about the husband's death!

It was months later that this came up, and our colleague could not understand why no one had called her or come to see her. Our boss even took all the cards we were going to send. This really hurt our colleague, and I still don't understand why my boss did this!

Snake bosses only see the people around them in light of how they might benefit the snake boss.

I recently had a boss who resided out of state. He would ask me to turn in all of my reports and strategies for marketing on a Tuesday so he could color code them and re-purpose my ideas for his boss on Thursday.

We were also asked to send him all of the marketing copy we wrote for new and exciting ideas to which his response always was, "Looks good. Go to print." I even sabotaged copy occasionally to see if he read it. The answer was no.

Instead of doing his job, he would make an Excel spreadsheet of how long it would take him to do the job at hand and show it to his boss to explain he did not have enough time. This man couldn't even explain to clients what he did. There wasn't a marketing term fancy enough for NOTHING!

Snake bosses may lie dormant in the sun for many days and even shed their skin, but those employees who survive remember that there is a snake boss within.

I used to work with a woman who was a control freak micromanager. I was in customer service and had to track air shipments off of flow sheets. Typically there were 9 lines of airbills and up to 30 sheets to track. We would call the airlines, confirm flights, and confirm deliveries.

This woman would take my flow sheets and use a RED pen to mark down EXACTLY what to do. One asterisk meant important. Three red asterisks and an exclamation meant jump on it. Never mind that I was one of the best CSR agents they had, she was relentless with me.

Then periodically she would grab my sheets and start randomly calling out shipments to get the status, and I would have to give her status on each one from MEMORY! I was always able to give her status which seemed to make her more aggressive. So then she started taking other CSR's sheets away from them and made ME mark their sheets with her red pen which, of course, made me look bad to my peers.

One day, my crazy manager was out smoking and an agent called that she was working on a problem with. I took the call and was fixing the problem when she came back and overheard me talking to him. She proceeded to tell me she had taken care of it (she didn't) and to get off the phone. I was in mid sentence when she took the phone off my ear, out of my hands, and slammed it down. I almost killed her.

She would also print out detailed phone lists of each extension and go line by line to make sure all the calls were business related.

Finally I couldn't take her anymore so I went part-time weekends and nights only (to get away from her) as I was having panic attacks because of her extreme behavior. I went to upper management, and they promoted me to week-end supervisor (to keep me from quitting) and let me change my shift to get away from her. Well THAT didn't work out

either as she started making personal attacks in the com-
ments in the computer, AND she would send me 50 e-mails
from home barking orders.

She was the sole reason for our high turnover in our
department, yet for some reason, she's still there to this day!

Finally after a deluge of people quit because of her
they took away her e-mailing privileges and prohibited her
from having any communication with the customer service
department. They demoted her and just put her in charge
of one account.

Once they cut her fangs, you could feel the tension
lift.

Snake boss's actions and behavior may seem
random and irrational. This is not the case. In order to
understand a snake boss, you must remember that they
only care about themselves and have no regard for other
people, except as those other people can be the means to
a desired end.

If you are forced to deal with a snake boss, everything must be presented in light of how it benefits, pro-
tects, or comforts the snake boss. Any other approach
will result in a venomous attack.

CHAPTER TWELVE

The Fish

Some people are so
dependent on an addiction
that it becomes their
entire world.

Fish are totally reliant on the water in which they live. They cannot imagine or relate to life outside the water.

Fish bosses see the world through a drunken, delusional haze. This affects their judgment and their actions.

When I first took this position, I found that the people who previously had this job left after one year. Only one person in the last 5 years has stayed longer than 16 months. I quickly realized why.

My boss finds it necessary to take 3-4 hour drinking lunches several times a week. After which, she returns to the office and imparts wisdom on what is wrong with the way I conduct business at my job and what I should do about it. This is delivered in a rather rabid fashion and very close to my face—allowing me to get the full affect of her alcohol use. I don't drink, so this is very offensive to me.

This manager has a friendship, outside of work, with the HR liaison to this office; so taking this to HR will only get me fired.

This is just the tip of the iceberg. I now see a therapist to deal with my feelings around how this manager treats me. There is complete disrespect to me as a person! This is a very bad manager. I've been a manager of 32 staff assistants in a government setting. I have never seen or experienced anything like this before.

Fish bosses do not exist in the workplace outside of their addiction. Even though a fish boss may be having a sober morning or even a sober two or three days, sooner or later you will deal with the addicted fish boss. A fish may live a brief time outside of water, but eventually, they have to get back to their accustomed environment.

A good day for a fish boss is only the calm before the storm unless they become willing to deal with their underlying problem and get the help they need.

Harry was a heavy drinker (liquid lunches every day). He was a Natural Gas Liquids Trader for a large oil company. Supposedly a great propane buy and sell trader.

I would type letters for his signature which were monthly price agreement letters and included a return approval signature line. He would sign on the approval line for the other company, not between the Sincerely and above his name. The letters were then ruined and I had to re-type them. This was before computers. I got where I tried to have

*them signed prior to lunch or went in and stood over him
and pointed where to sign.*

*Then one day he dropped his baggie of cocaine on
my desk accidentally. Boy, you should have seen his face
when I brought it to him!*

I never had much respect for this guy!

Dealing with a fish boss is much like dealing with
someone that is incapacitated or suffers from a mental
illness. No matter how talented or qualified the fish boss
may be to do their job when sober, you will be forced to
deal with an overall body of work that reflects their di-
minished capacity.

You may feel empathetic for your fish boss's disease or the conditions under which they try to function;
however, you cannot separate yourself from their addiction while you're in the workplace.

You might realize that a friend has had too much
to drink and even feel sorry for them in their condition;
however, you wouldn't let them get behind the wheel of
your car and drive away.

Unfortunately, if you are associated with a fish
boss, you are riding in their proverbial car, and they are
functionally asleep at the wheel. It's only a matter of time
until there will be a fatality accident.

I have had some very good bosses and some not so good ones, but I think the worst boss I ever had was at my first real job.

I was a senior in high school working in an ice cream shop that also had a gas station/convenience store on the other side. It was really a very sad story. The owners were a married couple. She was the sweetest, kindest person you would ever want to meet. Business was business, but she still took the time to show that she really cared for her employees. Unfortunately, he was just the opposite. He was an alcoholic who was in denial of his problem and would not seek help. He would slip cans of beer into his pocket from the cooler in the other side of the store and hide them in the medicine cabinet in his office. What he failed to re-alize was that every time he opened or closed the medicine cabinet, it could be heard throughout the building.

We were all aware of the problem, because typi-cally after he had a drink, he would get in one of his moods and have an anger episode. We could hear when she begged him not to drink, but she was unsuccessful in her attempts.

As a teenager just entering the workforce, this was not the type of environment that I desired or needed to be subjected to. The day after Christmas that year, his loving wife had a massive heart attack and died. Going to work after her death was very difficult. There was no one to buffer his anger and no one to accommodate for his disease and no one to share care and concern. I resigned right after graduation.

We spend the larger portion of our week in the workplace. Our coworkers are a part of our extended family. When one hurts or has a problem, everyone shares in the pain and issues that arise.

In today's world, we have the benefit of employee assistance programs. Unfortunately, thirty years ago that was not an option. Perhaps the saddest part of all was that a few years later I picked up a newspaper and read his obituary. The word on the street was that he had drank himself to death.

Worst boss, sad end!

Unlike other bad bosses, when you're dealing with a fish boss, there are no winners, and everybody is a loser. The disease that the fish boss is dealing with affects everyone in the work environment.

There are support groups for family members and friends of alcoholics and addicts. The people who have organized these support groups recognize while you may have only one alcoholic or addict in the circle, everyone is affected and suffers from the ravages of the disease.

It could be argued that all bad bosses need help of some type, but fish bosses need a very specific kind of help. For your sake, the sake of your organization, and even for the sake of the fish boss, you've got to take action.

First, you must document the behavior in a factual, unemotional manner. Then, ideally, you should confront the fish boss with other members of management or colleagues in attendance who have observed the same behavior. You should never be judgmental or accusatory, but merely point out how the fish boss behavior is affecting coworkers, clients, and the entire organization.

If your intervention is unsuccessful, you have nothing to lose, because—with a fish boss at the helm—the organizational ship is destined to end up on the rocks. On the other hand, you might just save your job, along with everyone else's, and you could save a life in the process.

CHAPTER THIRTEEN

The Peacock

An inflated ego is God's
gift to small people.

A peacock is a fairly modest and unremarkable bird until they extend their colorful feathers to create a façade of beauty. The image is attractive to look at but offers no substance or practicality.

Peacock bosses are wearing rose colored glasses as they gaze into a mirror in order to observe themselves. No one can live up to the opinion that peacock bosses have of themselves.

I had a boss who put in 10 to 16 hour days on a regular basis. Without saying it, his body language said he was better than—and worked harder than—anyone.

As his direct report I had to go to him when problems arose. I always hated having to go to his office. Out of respect, not wanting to interrupt his line of thinking, I would stand in the door waiting for him to see me and respond at a convenient moment. That approach didn't work. He just ignored me. If I would knock, the standard response was a fist to the desk in disgust that he had been interrupted. I struggled with this for years. Honestly, I wouldn't bother him if I could figure things out myself.

Finally—realizing that my job was my choice—I found the power to rise above his outbursts to keep a positive outlook.

He has long since moved on, and I am still here.

Peacock bosses often confuse fear and intimidation for respect. Their inflated, self-important image allows them to look down upon everyone else, often from a faulty, perverse position.

I was working as an HR Manager for a large US based automotive parts supplier that has since closed the doors.

For the first time in my life, I actually contacted the Human Rights Commission and lodged a formal complaint. This individual although a well-educated and knowledgeable senior manager (operations manager overseeing two facilities located in Canada) was unbelievable. For the purpose of this story I will refer to him as Charlie. He was demeaning, intimidating, obnoxious and downright rude to employees at all levels reporting to him.

I think the worst situation (one of many) was when, during a meeting with local management, he singled out an individual of Polish descent and began interrogating him about a maintenance issue on a heating oven in one of the plants. When the individual responded that they

pretty much encapsulates the ego Arrogance had that he was untouchable even by the Almighty.

From that point forward, Arrogance managed based on his previous accomplishments, pointing out his past decisions were always correct and must be applied his way for whatever decisions lay ahead of us. His decisions on providing service to our customers and our clients was always secondary to whether or not it agreed with his thought process.

Arrogance was always right, even if it meant a loss of customer loyalty or employee integrity. Arrogance also yelled and intimidated his employees to get it done "Or else I'm going to have to find someone else who will do it my way." This led to upper level executives literally bribing government officials for business favors and our company offending the likes of state senators.

Of course, Arrogance always denied any involvement in our company scandals. He would never conduct business that way.

To this day, Arrogance still holds his position, makes high senior executive pay, and manages with an unyielding grip.

Peacock bosses not only make poor leaders but poor people as well. They aren't fun to be around personally or professionally.

If you're forced to deal with a peacock boss, your only hope is to explain how the proper course of action that you're recommending will make the peacock boss look good. You can hardly overplay this card, because that which you feel to be ridiculously undeserved flattery, the peacock boss will view as reality.

CHAPTER FOURTEEN

The Skunk

Some people only annoy
those in the immediate
vicinity, while others
pollute the entire environment.

Nothing is more distinctive and disgusting than the smell of a skunk. It's hard to know exactly where the skunk might be, because their awful aroma seems to be everywhere.

Skunk bosses exhibit behaviors and characteristics that can infect an entire organization.

I began working for a company in its start-up phase. I worked several jobs as needed, and both the owner and general manager complimented me on my work ethic and job performance.

I worked two years in the payroll and accounting offices for this company when the owner's mother took over operations and fired the general manager. At this time, she brought me into the office and told me she had no idea how I could have handled the job I was doing, because I was stupid and ill-qualified. She also told me that she would have never hired me for the job, and if I messed up—just once—I would be let go.

When I would do a job well, she accepted that as what I was being paid to do, even when I went above and beyond to achieve results or make processes flow better. On the other hand, when I would make a mistake or have to ask her a question about my job, she would tell me that if I did not know then I was incompetent, and that there were many other people she could hire for my job.

I was not sure what my job description was, because when the owner was in charge I was human resources manager. I helped interview to hire and handled all of the paperwork. When the owner's mother took over, I no longer worked with employees on their issues because she said I was too mushy and gave them too much leeway. I did continue to handle all of the other paperwork (i.e., insurance, employees files, unemployment, insurance, etc).

When an employee would bring an issue to me, I was not allowed to handle it and was told my job was payroll clerk. Accordingly, when bonuses came out, I received the same amount as the people on the floor because she said I was not a manager, and did not handle anything more than the people on the floor did.

The last straw was when she wanted me to falsify records to unemployment for former employees because she said they did not deserve unemployment, and she did not want to pay it.

I know that she is still handling businesses for her son, but I am very happy not to have to go to work every day wondering what she would find to fault me with today.

It is very difficult, if not impossible, to avoid a skunk boss. No matter where you turn, you discover that their stench has preceded you.

My boss hit at least 85% of the 10 characteristics of a bad boss. He redefined micromanaging!

He gave me little, if any, guidelines for tasks then blew me out of the water OR ignored me for literally days (which is no small feat when you sit less than 50 ft apart!)

The best part was the ending! He let me go via a TEXT message on a Sunday!! Seriously! I had NO idea, no calm before the storm. It was November 1, and he texted me.

After six years of loyal service! I have NEVER been so insulted in all of my life! And if separation of service is not enough, he actually emailed me a few weeks later to see how I was and if we could go have beers!

Karma works in mysterious ways. I am now happily employed in a much better position where I am respected and appreciated and actually like my boss and coworkers!

A skunk boss's behavior will smell the worst when they are dealing with an awkward task such as firing someone. The type of thinking that allows a skunk boss to terminate someone via text message can adversely affect an entire workplace.

To begin with I hate sales.

My boss wants me to be manipulative and blames me if I make a call and get a voicemail. He swears nonstop.

A woman today (Monday) had to leave because her daughter got sent to the ER for a roofing accident and he said, "Why couldn't this happen yesterday? It's just a slip." And this was not in a joking manner.

I have been here two weeks, and I already plan on quitting. I've never met someone so rude, disrespectful, and belittling.

A skunk boss will not only mishandle a personal emergency that a team member is facing. They will do it in such a way that makes the entire organization stink. Everyone understands that if the skunk boss will do something despicable to one of my colleagues, then they will eventually do it to me.

Just a few months into my first full-time professional position, I caught one of our interns plagiarizing an article that would run in national newspapers. That made me suspicious of her previous work, and I discovered that one of the articles she had written that ran in several papers was heavily plagiarized.

I took this information to my supervisor at the time, who also supervised the interns. His response was to have me confront her about it instead of him, despite my utter inexperience and lack of any authority. I then had to encourage her to step down voluntarily.

I didn't feel like it should be voluntary at all, and because she was using the internship for school credit I felt like it should be reported to the school.

Despite the fact that the supervisor was an adjunct professor at the same school, he refused to report the incident and instructed me to give neutral references for the intern if anyone called down the line for a reference check. I understand that you have to be careful these days when letting people go due to the prevalence of lawsuits, but in this case we had a clear, unarguable reason for letting her go, especially since her actions could have resulted in lawsuits against us by the people she plagiarized.

The supervisor tried to write the incident off as a learning experience for me, but really he just didn't want to confront her and put that on me.

Skunk bosses are often absent when there's a difficult task facing the team. They would rather leave it to someone else to deal with terminations and other difficult tasks.

Even though the skunk boss may not be present, their smell lingers.

The worst boss I ever had was a former city manager who made every department head's work life miserable. He walked in the door with an attitude of mistrust; basically we were all in the red and had to earn our way into the black, i.e. his trust.

He was a very short man and enjoyed getting right in front of your face to make his points, finger poking toward your nose!

In retrospect, he never should have been hired because—in a 21 year city manager career—he had never stayed anywhere longer than three years and most cities averaged two years (the same as the life of his contracts). He lasted exactly two years here. I believe we were his twelfth job in 21 years.

Before starting work, a mandate was sent to our interim city manager for each department head to prepare a very detailed report about their department(s) which included personnel, goals, accomplishments, etc. We obliged and created detailed handbooks to encompass all of these particulars. He asked me several questions his first month or so on the job, which I answered, but also told him that the information was in my book. He brushed me away saying he hadn't looked at any of them!

His first act of callousness was to exile our beloved assistant city manager to an out building just overseeing planning and zoning. This ACM had been here 11 years at the time, knew the history of our city inside and out, and had a tremendous passion for our city.

On one occasion, the husband of my administrative assistant came to him complaining that his wife was having an affair and that I, her boss, was letting her leave during the day to meet her boyfriend. He entertained this husband privately for an hour, then came to my office to threaten my job if this is true and forced me to listen to the husband for half an hour. Then, he called my administrative assistant to his office and allowed the husband to verbally berate her for another 30 minutes. She just sat silently before being told to provide documents to substantiate every absence she had from work! Thankfully, this situation defused quickly and was never mentioned again.

Another department head and I were made examples of via time sheets, which exempt staff should not be required to complete. He frequently changed our timesheets without advance notice or our permission, causing our city to face potential Department of Labor retribution.

As his two year anniversary drew near, at least two of us approached council members—which is a huge no-no—to express our fear for the future of our city and wonderful, valued city staff who were mostly all looking for other jobs. He was gone within three weeks. They were very grateful to those who spoke up, and I'm very happy to say that our wonderful assistant city manager was immediately promoted, and we are thriving under the past two years of her leadership.

Every group reflects its leadership. If you have been in the presence of a skunk, only time will diminish and completely eliminate the odor. Skunk bosses must be removed in order to air out the entire organization.

Only when ownership or upper management fully understand the pollution that a single skunk boss is creating can there be peace, cooperation, and an environment where everyone can breathe easily.

The Skunk

CHAPTER FIFTEEN

The Chameleon

We can learn to work and
even thrive alongside
people with whom we
disagree or have differences
of opinion; however, this
becomes impossible if they
are continually changing.

The chameleon is a fascinating creature. It has the ability to change its color to match its environment. In this way, it can appear to blend in or hide anywhere.

Chameleon bosses are dangerous and unpredictable. You quite simply never know who you're dealing with.

As senior vice president of operations, I reported to the executive vice president of one of the top 10 cable telecommunications companies. This individual was probably one of the finest financial minds in the cable industry at the time but also the most mean-spirited person that I had ever met.

In public settings, she was always very friendly and positioned herself as the savior of the company since she had come in to assist with a turnaround. Behind the scenes she was ruthless. I stayed and reported to her way too long, nine years. I watched her target anyone who questioned her. Once targeted, she would belittle the individual in staff meetings or ignore them at the conference table as if they did not exist.

One day, I got a call from a colleague telling me to watch out. On a quarterly basis we were requested to come to a meeting at the corporate office for a general staff meeting with the other senior VPs. During this particular meeting she asked me if I was ready to make my presentation. I asked which presentation she was referring to. She told me everyone else was prepared. When I told her that no one had informed me that she had expected a specific presentation, she ignored me for the rest of the meeting. She then avoided my emails and would not return calls.

I was being reelected as a board member of our state wide trade organization. She arranged the prior evening to have someone else elected to the position but didn't inform me until five minutes prior to the board luncheon. Shortly thereafter, I resigned my position with the company with six months' notice, after 17 years of excellent service. Ironically she was fired a month later.

A number of my colleagues called me to inform me that I should now stay with the company. No, I'd had it with that organization.

Chameleon bosses can be forced to change their colors, but remember: You can't rely on this, because their color can change back in the blink of an eye.

I was an assistant to an administrator who was transferred. Her replacement was promoted from within our organization. As she knew little about the program, she left me in charge of daily operations, while she attended meetings, public performances, etc.

When problems developed due to lack of leadership, she gave me a devastatingly insulting and untruthful evaluation. I was called into her boss's office while he delivered the crushing evaluation. I disputed the allegations, and they called her in, but she backed down when she had to face me and could not support her facts.

I worked for her for several more years, and she continued to give me more and more of the responsibility, but I could never trust her evaluations.

A woman in London experienced the heartache and turmoil of dealing with a chameleon boss.

How about having a boss who tells you at every opportunity, "Do you know how much I earn?"

I worked for a private security company, and from the interview stage was warned about the boss. Even the recruitment agency called me five times before the interview with her, to brief me about this woman who was "intimidating and very demanding." Just before my interview with her, the HR manager of the company gave me a final tip. "She's very particular. She likes straight answers, so you have to answer direct and quick answers."

"Whatever," I thought.

My own personal philosophy is: How can you be intimidated by someone/something you've not experienced personally? And why on earth should I change my natural behaviour at interviews to appease this one particular person? She either liked me for who I am or not—as simple as that.

At the interview, I was myself and ended up getting the job as head of communications. A year later almost to the day, I left—fourth within three years to have left the position I filled!

I reported directly to this lady, who as she said in my interview as part of her introduction, "I am half Italian and half Croatian. I am single and I like to have a lot of men. No kidding!"

At the time I thought this was funny and blushy, and I was drawn to it. But I should have been more savvy, as in time I came to see what everyone in the organisation warned me about—that woman was the devil incarnate.

She would literally rule by terrorising everyone around her. Even the head of the US office and former Under Secretary of State in America was petrified of this poor excuse of a woman. At my weekly meetings with her, she would slowly manipulate me by "confiding" in me *things that my colleagues would say about me, and I discovered later, she would do the same to others.*

She never tired of reminding me that I was honoured to be given five minutes of her precious time. "Do you know how much I earn?" I have no idea how many times I had to endure this humiliating game, but I have to admit it ended up breaking me down.

She would come into a room and start screaming at the receptionist because she did not have the right shoes on, or scream at the Global Head of Corporate in front of everyone, because he chose to use an Apple mouse instead of the standard HP mouse, as it fit better in his hand.

She would scream at the HR Director, a 62 year old Scottish sweetie, with her pitch reaching such levels that even the water tanks would start to vibrate. He left midway during my tenure, without so much as an announcement being made, thanking him for his loyal and tireless work over the last three years with the company.

Last time I saw him (I was transferred from London to Dubai) was just before he disappeared from the company (that's what would happen to people. They would just "disappear." Indeed, I ended up "disappearing"), and he was a broken man.

Devil Wears Prada??? This woman was 100,000 times worse. During our weekly meetings, she would force me to read emails from her lovers and get me to reply to them as her written English was not perfect.

She would call me into her office and berate me for an hour, accusing me of flirting with the CEO. She caught me leaning over his desk once because I was going through some corporate work images that were on my laptop, and she accused me of leaning towards him in a seductive manner. Nothing could be further from the truth. She spends all her time playing games, pitting one employee against the other, and terrorising everyone.

Sometimes when chameleon bosses change their colors, it can be frustrating and painful. Other times, you just find out there's no such thing as a free lunch, or even dinner.

We had just been assigned a new director of marketing communications that was based out of state.

On his first trip to town, he invited the four of us out for a nice dinner in the downtown area. After a wonderful dinner and several drinks later, the bill came. It was one of those awkward moments when the server placed the bill in the middle of the table, and we all looked around nonchalantly as if we didn't see it.

After a few minutes we realized he wasn't picking it up. One of our team members decided to break the uncomfortable silence and said, "Do you want me to pick this up?"

I knew her card was close to the max due to a trade show she had recently expensed, so I offered to pick it up.

He said, "Sure, I'll sign off on it tomorrow."

Well, we came to find out that he wasn't as far up the chain as he appeared and had no signing authority. I had to expense it and explain why I took our team out for dinner and why the company should reimburse me for a $650 bill!

When you first start working with a chameleon boss, it is easy to believe that the inconsistencies are only in your head, but after enough time passes, it becomes painfully obvious that it's not in your head. It's in their character.

My "bad boss" would constantly contradict himself in what he said and did. Our company was in a continual state of confusion. I discounted this at first as a communication error or thought that maybe my boss wasn't able to remember everything he said.

After this confusion persisted for months and I saw him continuously outright lie to other people, I realized it was not me or the other employees' fault for being confused. It was my boss purposely being dishonest with others.

There should never be constant confusion in a work environment. Be truthful and consistent with your co-workers and your clients. By being earnestly and sincerely honest, people will like working for you, doing business with you, and referring you to others.

Many types of bad bosses make it advisable for you to document everything. Chameleon bosses make it imperative. The documentation cannot just be your recollections, recorded in your own files since these can be disputed, and the chameleon boss can change colors while fabricating a string of lies.

Only when enough people observe the color of a chameleon boss and witness the inevitable change will the chameleon boss lose their power.

The Chameleon

CHAPTER SIXTEEN

The Vulture

Some see those around them as people needing to be fed, while lesser people can only see those around them as food.

Vultures feed off of other animals that are dead or dying. There is something almost noble about one healthy animal stalking and pursuing another, but vultures live off of the pain and suffering of others.

Vulture bosses do not understand or seek win/win scenarios. Vulture bosses believe they can only win when everyone else loses.

I couldn't believe my ears! My boss told me, "The last thing I'd do would be to promote someone smarter than me."

He went on to talk about how his goal was to continue to get promoted, so he didn't want to help anyone else who might be perceived as being smarter than himself, because that person might get a desired promotion ahead of him! And we wouldn't want that, would we!

Rarely are vulture bosses obvious and forthcoming with their intentions. Their carnivorous behavior is simply instinctual and part of their nature.

Then there are the vulture bosses that remind us all that we are only food for them. Anything outside of the workplace is just a distraction that could interrupt their meal.

My worst boss repeatedly said, "If you have a life outside the company, you are stealing from the organization."

In my family, there arose a possible situation where my nephew could be lost to foster care. He lived in a city 1,000 miles away. I did not want my irresponsible sibling to know that I was willing to step in and take custody of my nephew, instead of me sitting back and allowing them to slip away to foster care. I was very concerned that if the irresponsible sibling found out I was willing to step in, that they would abdicate all responsibility for their child, and ignore their responsibility. Aged relatives, who could not take custody of my nephew, kept me informed of the court dates and possible last minute attorney negotiations.

I was informed on a Monday night that the court date was set for Wednesday, and that the attorneys might work something out Tuesday. If they did not work things out, my nephew would likely be put in foster care at the Wednesday hearing.

The next morning, I told my boss that I might get a phone call anytime that day and have to head straight to the airport in order to fly the 1,000 miles in time to walk into the courthouse to adopt my nephew the next day.

His response was one sentence, "What about your commitments here?"

I paused, hoping and thinking he would clarify it with possibly something soft like, "Can you prepare others to handle your projects?"

I waited, and he said, "How would he impact your commitments here?"

I knew from previous statements, that he knew me having custody of my nephew would mean an end to my 70 hour work weeks and two to four airline flights per week of travel.

My boss got up and walked away. He expected me to be there not just 40 hours per week, but 70 or more. I felt like he thought my adopting my nephew was just like stealing his bonus and pay raise, and also stealing from the company.

In the eyes of vulture bosses, employees only have value to the extent they fuel and provide sustenance for the vulture boss.

In hindsight, I should have never accepted a job from a woman who looked exactly like the Wicked Witch of the West minus the green skin.

After a few months in my new role, people realized I responded faster and friendlier than my manager. When people began to bypass her and came to me for help is when things changed. She made the comment, "They should be coming to me, NOT you." Even though as she said it, we both knew when they brought her a request, she told me to handle it, provide her the answer, and she took the credit.

She began having nearly daily feedback sessions with me. This feedback (I use the term loosely) was always negative and stretched the truth significantly.

On one occasion, she informed me I took too long for lunch. She could only provide one example. The date she provided was the day I used my lunch break for a dentist appointment, of which she had advanced knowledge. I was gone an hour and 15 minutes. It's also worth mentioning I normally worked 7:30 a.m. to 6:00 p.m. and rarely took a lunch.

Then there was the proofreading. After six months in the role, I was no longer allowed to send an offer letter without her approval. Interestingly enough, the offer letter was a standardized template; however, with each template I provided her, out came the red pen and the hacking commenced. Granted, I do not profess to be a proficient writer, but I can complete a standardized template.

After 16 long months of being bullied and degraded by her, and crying to and from work most days, I left. I overcame the mental damage she inflicted and regained my confidence. Now as a department head, I remember the things she would say and do to me, and I vow every day to be the opposite.

Vulture bosses rarely trust anyone. Their greatest fear is that they will end up as just another part of the food chain.

My last employer was the worst boss ever.

First, he did not trust any of his employees and would double check their work no matter what it was; and you had to check every repair with him so he could okay the repair, or he would tell you that you were wrong and to redo it.

Second, he had a lunch rule that lunches were taken between 12:00 to 1:00 every day. If you were at a customer's site working on some equipment, you would have to pack up your tools and drive back to the shop, take lunch and then drive back to finish the job.

Third, he would call you out in front of the other employees and tell you what a worthless person you were. He would also do this to his wife and the service manager as well.

Fourth, he would from time to time follow you to jobs to make sure that you were taking the route that he wanted you to take.

Fifth, he would check your tool bag to make sure you were not taking parts home with you. Not all the time—just spot checks as he called them.

Sixth, time off from work is on "your dime not mine."

I hated to get up and go to work everyday, because I just knew it would be more of the same. I felt like the fox caught in a trap in the woods. He eats his own foot off to get away from the trap.

True vulture bosses only see subordinates as a smorgasbord; therefore, they never assist or help anyone. Vulture bosses are confused and frustrated when employees attempt to cooperate with one another or exhibit traits of teamwork.

I was helping a younger analyst with the details of his first log physical, which we did at least quarterly. Shortly thereafter, I was called into my boss's office, and with the door open, was chewed out very loudly about me helping the new analyst, and that he was supposed to figure it out for himself. When I mentioned I thought this was a team, and we should all help each other out, she screamed that if he screwed up then that was his fault, and it was not my business, and I was told to do only my own job.

I sat there and took the abuse. As I left, the young analyst was just outside of the door, not in view, but had obviously heard the whole thing. I apologized to him for hearing that, and decided to take the rest of the day off.

If you avoid being eaten by a vulture boss and survive the encounter, you can actually live to fight another day and even thrive in the future.

My worst boss ever taught me how to treat employees when I was the boss.

I was the only report to this particular boss. She came in at 9:00 a.m., left at 3:30 p.m. and gave me enough work that I had to often stay until 9-10 p.m. In addition, she required me to do odd jobs at her house while on the clock.

I soon realized that instead of being a victim, I could learn from the situation. Her ineffective management forced me to learn to be self-sufficient, innovative, and a life-long learner. Looking back on it, she made me a better person, all inadvertently, of course.

If you're dealing with a vulture boss, it is impossible to get them to stop looking upon you as food; however, if you can demonstrate that cooperative teamwork can keep everyone well fed, you can succeed.

Those people who raise chickens come to understand that you can eat chicken for one meal or enjoy eggs permanently.

Vulture bosses have become victims of their own limited world view. If you can help them understand that everyone can win, you will begin to observe positive changes in your vulture boss.

CHAPTER SEVENTEEN

The Porcupine

It is good when we can
reach out to one another,
but there are some people
you cannot touch without
injuring yourself.

Some animals defend themselves by fighting back while others flee. Porcupines roll up into a ball, exposing painful quills to anyone that approaches them.

Porcupine bosses seem to stab and stick everyone in the operation—sometimes, for no other reason than the fact that they can.

I was working a temp to perm job at a manufacturing company in the North Carolina Mountains right after they had a merger. I was one of two HR Generalists for 800 people. I knew something was up when the other Generalist and assistant would go outside to smoke and talk under their breath about the boss.

One day, the boss told me to post a job description on Monster "BY THE END OF THE DAY," she said squinting her eyes and shaking her finger. I got on it but couldn't find the job description anywhere. I asked everyone in my vicinity with no luck. So I replied to all on an email where she also requested I post the job. (She said she was unavailable all day and left.)

Finally by the end of the day someone, somewhere helped me. I was just a month into the job. Then the boss came into the office and started screaming at me for the email, saying a VP was on that list and I had no business emailing him! There was no chance to even explain my thinking or challenges in getting the job done on time.

The other people in the office (yes, it was a public whipping) lowered their heads in horror. When she left, they said how sorry they were. But that day was freedom day for me. I declared I didn't deserve a job like that and the next day I told the boss we needed to plan my exit because I can't do my best work here.

I really wanted to tell her off, but I figured her Emotional Quotient was so low, she wouldn't get it!

There is simply no way to get close to a porcupine boss without getting stabbed. It is human nature to want to reach out to the person deep inside, but a porcupine boss just won't let you connect.

My very worst boss turned out to be the one I learned my most valuable lesson from.

I was employed by a financial planning firm. My boss was a woman who frightened grown men. No one would ever ride on the elevator with her, and she would knit during our staff meetings, and she always had to sit at the head of the table. In the beginning, I wanted to quit every day.

She asked me to run reports, and actually sketched out what information she wanted in what columns in Excel (including column width) and when I gave her EX-ACTLY what she asked for, my work was called garbage to my face. She was never a warm fuzzy boss, always cold and distant. I thought I had a pretty thick skin considering I worked on a Marine Corps base before going to work for her, but tough Marines were nothing compared to working for that woman.

Marines are tough people that do a tough job, but there may be no more caring, giving team members than Marines. Porcupine bosses act tough on the outside for no reason and without benefit to anyone.

A few years ago I worked for the WORST boss. For about four years, I was a barista for a locally owned and operated thriving coffee stand.

Luckily, I did not have to work with the owner more than two times a year, but when I did it was hell! She would drop things off once a week and come in screaming and cussing for no reason, but every now and then she felt the need to ask us how we were doing. The problem with this is, as soon as someone started to answer she would walk away.

I worked my way up to the busiest stand after a few months, and she had me working mornings with the manager. I covered shifts, would come in early, would stay late, you name it. One term of college I had to work evenings because of the classes I had to take, but she told me she needed me to work mornings and that I needed to quit going to college. After that ridiculous comment, I told her I would not be able to do that so she told me I would only be put on weekends. Well, weekends would not support my finances so I got a week night job. After that she was mad at me for a few months.

On one particular day, I was working the 4:00 a.m. shift and was five minutes late to work. Rather than taking the chance of her finding out, I decided to call her around 9:00 a.m. Honesty is the best policy right? Wrong!

She seemed fine on the phone saying she needed to write me up and I agreed. About 1:00 p.m., she showed up and gave me the write-up slip, which I signed and I headed out the door to an appointment but was then stopped by her. She had me turn in all my keys and told me I was fired.

Not to mention a few years before when one night when I called her at 9:00 p.m. saying I had to get my shift covered the next morning due to an excruciating pain in my kidneys (which I thought was my lower back). She told me I wasn't allowed to get anyone to cover it. At 1:30 a.m.,

I called her from the emergency room after being rushed in for a kidney infection, and she said I still needed to go to work. This was also after my dad had talked to her. Being the loyal employee I am, I went in at 4:00 a.m. and opened the stand, after being out of the hospital for one hour. At that point I was accused of being out all night partying, even though I had a release note.

I think I had the worst boss!

A young lady in Alberta, Canada, discovered that the satisfaction of a job well done can be totally destroyed by a few prickly words from a porcupine boss.

I worked for two years in an engineering department. At that time a microfilming system was being installed to preserve the old plant drawings that were falling apart. My job was to film the drawings and to redraw some of the oldest drawings which would then be used as samples for the new system.

Upon finishing the project, my boss stated, "I'm glad you did such a good job on the drawings, because I can now tell the guys if a dumb girl can do it this way, so can they."

I went on to be the owner of a company with a staff of 30 who I treat very respectfully.

Porcupine bosses will discriminate against certain groups of people, but they are willing to stab everyone with their painful quills on an equal opportunity basis.

The worst boss I ever had was a director of HR.

He spent his first week on the job meeting with only one group of minority/protected class hourly employees and asking them if they felt discriminated against. He never met with any other groups.

During investigations he would first ask the race of the employees involved—not the details of the investigation.

Finally, he told me I was expected to work more hours than my co-manager because I was single and had no children.

Porcupine bosses make life miserable for everyone. If you have a deep and mutually respectful relationship with someone, you can stand it when it may get a bit prickly between you; but a porcupine boss creates an atmosphere in which no one can get close, and the only personal exchange will be the stab of a painful quill.

If you need to confront a porcupine boss, it is best to do so immediately after one of their useless quills stabs you. Then calmly say, "Mr. Porcupine Boss, I realize you wouldn't say something like that simply to hurt me, so there must be something you want me to learn from this so I can improve in the future. Please help me understand how I should take your comments or actions in this situation in order to improve my performance."

A porcupine boss will never change unless they are exposed for the petty tyrants they are. If you can sincerely and respectfully approach them with your desire to learn and improve, there may be a light at the end of the tunnel.

CHAPTER EIGHTEEN

The Tiger

True leaders never feel the
need to prove their power
to anyone. They know they
have it.

The tiger may be the most terrifying animal in the jungle. Tigers are sleek, swift, ruthless killing machines.

Tiger bosses have not really earned their stripes, so they exert their power out of their own feelings of inadequacy.

I had a boss that was great if you were on her good side. The moment you did something wrong though, watch out!

She was a surgeon and—needless to say—a perfectionist. She punched me (gave me a black eye more than once); took hemostats during an operation and clamped them on my hands; took a retractor (heavy gauge steel) and smacked my hands. Not to mention, fired me on a daily basis but expected me to come to work and work 20 hours a day continually.

Things are tough enough in the operating room without having to deal with an enraged tiger boss. It almost makes you feel like you need to bring your own anesthetic.

I was working as a manager for an organization about 10 years ago. In an all-hands staff meeting, the CEO put up an organizational chart and told everyone to find their names and verify that it was, indeed, in the right place. He gave us all about 10 minutes to do that. There were around 175 people in the company. Everyone was joking and having a good time during the exercise.

After the 10 minutes were up, he put up another organizational chart and said, "Okay, now everyone find your name on this chart. If you can't find your name, that means you no longer work here!"

Well, you could have heard the proverbial pin drop in that conference room. No one moved, so he took the chart off the wall, walked to each person, and said, "Can you find your name? No? Well then, leave immediately." The next person. "Can you find your name? Yes? Then get back to work."

About 50 people were actually fired that day, but about 90 of us walked out the door.

I've heard it said that tigers eat their young. Well, it's certain that tiger bosses eat their employees and seem to enjoy the process.

I was a 14-year employee of a major auto insurance carrier. For the last 10 years, I had been one of 30 employees selected to start an elite new department from the ground up. It became very successful and the pivotal department for our organization.

We had always been a collegial group of team players leaving our egos outside and focusing our energy on ensuring that policies and procedures were in the best interests of the department, throwing out what didn't work, and keeping in what did. The motto always being: hard on ideas, soft on people.

In 2007, there was a major shift at the top of the food chain, and all new upper management was brought in to run our department, including a woman who became my direct supervisor, who I will call Y.

This was a woman who had been with the company for almost 30 years but had absolutely no clue about this department. She brought in most of her own people to do her bidding—right, wrong, or otherwise—and she and I locked horns instantly.

Because she had no idea what the procedures were and was too insecure to ask, she would wait until I had completed a requested project and then tell me that she liked the way her own people had done it better and that I had to redo mine. When I advised I had done the project according to policy, she told me she didn't care and that she was in charge now!

Tiger bosses are territorial. They feel compelled to hunt and stalk everything in their territory, even in situations where their tactics are most inappropriate.

My worst boss was an extreme micromanager who was viewed by most of her employees as a tyrant. This micromanager demanded to dictate almost every action of her direct reports both at work and within the community.

As the focus of the organization was to provide counseling and healing for victims of domestic violence which results from power and control issues, the irony of the dysfunction of the organization proved to be a huge learning experience.

Some predators hunt and kill only to survive while others do it because it is their nature. Tiger bosses actually enjoy the process. They go out of their way to terrorize.

Our company experienced its first employee layoffs just a few months after a new vice president was hired.

He had the dreaded task of selecting the individuals and informing them of their fate. He selected one of the highest performing sales managers to be laid off for reasons unknown to the staff. It was a devastating blow to the staff, and it was a very emotional situation.

The laid off worker was escorted to her office by the HR staff and was given boxes to pack her belongings as they monitored her actions. The staff was crushed over this loss, and they were all understandably concerned about their own jobs.

About two months later, the VP decided he would meet with all members of the staff individually to get to know them better. After meeting with the very first staff member (who was an entry level employee), he thought it would be funny to send her back to her desk—right in the middle of the department—with an empty box! What a moron! This entry level employee politely told the VP that she didn't think the staff would find that very funny.

He kept insisting that she take the box and even went so far as to get a box from the storage area and tried to force her to take it. But she expertly deflected his insistence and walked out without the box!! NOT FUNNY!

Tiger bosses are ruthless. They are cruel and vicious. They see everyone around them only as prey to be dominated and devoured.

So here it goes, my introduction to Heat/Ventilation/Air Conditioning. I am desperate for work by the time I come upon an entry level HVAC job. I quickly take it. Not glamorous work. Going into crawl spaces, attics, and many other confined dirty places. Hard work and only starts at minimum wage.

Shortly thereafter, the son of the owner takes over the company. In the first 3 months, I saw most of the employees leave. I saw this as my opportunity to advance.

I quickly moved myself into a lead position. Six weeks green, I am running a truck teaching myself a trade with no help from my employer. I manage to pick up/learn/excel at this demanding trade.

First year was great, even though the average employee would quit after about 3 weeks because they couldn't keep the pace for pay. Seemed to be I was training a new face every other week.

I managed to increase my wages by two-thirds. I felt I had a good relationship with my boss, even though nobody else liked him for various reasons I would soon discover first hand.

I then injured my back through no fault of my own. Guess the 12 hour days 6 days a week finally caught up with me. Not only was I forced to break my work limitations, I was still expected to produce as if I was 100 percent while training a new employee.

When I told him I needed time to get better and refused to violate my doctor's orders, he laid me off work. Then when I came back, he had dropped my wages one-third and found myself being treated poorly along with *accommodations that allow me to get my work done not available for me yet still available to other employees.*

Feeling this was wrong, unethical, and borderline illegal I left for other employment.

Knowing a few people that still worked there, I heard stories and witnessed other employees getting fired for things such as taking emergency leaves for family deaths, being hospitalized, and other major events that anyone with an ounce of compassion would understand. For instance, one person called in with bleeding ulcers and was in the hospital, and the boss says to that, "Oh, does someone's tummy hurt so they can't make it to work?" then hung up the phone. When he tried to return to work the following day he was fired.

Tiger bosses are among the most difficult to deal with. Their drive, determination, and tenacity have made them successful, but when turned inward on the organization, it can be deadly.

When dealing with a tiger boss, you must find respectful ways to redirect their power and ferocity toward your organization's competition and the challenges you are facing in the marketplace. If a tiger boss has a challenge, he will often rise to the occasion, but without sufficient prey in the marketplace jungle, he will simply begin to attack and devour his own young.

CHAPTER NINETEEN

The Shrew

Some people are naturally
annoying and unintentionally
rub others the wrong way,
but occasionally, you find
someone who is so
obnoxious they actually enjoy
spreading the misery.

The shrew is known to be whiney, suspicious, scheming, paranoid, and stingy. This is unpleasant in the animal kingdom but unbearable in the workplace.

Shrew bosses display all of the characteristics we would reject in our personal lives. Unfortunately, when you have a shrew boss at work, it can ruin your professional life.

Back in 1999, my husband's job transferred him to another state. The biggest challenge I thought I would have to overcome would be helping my two children—then ages 10 and 11—adjust to life going from a city of 40,000 to a city with almost a million people. Never in my wildest dreams would I have ever thought that I would be facing one of the biggest challenges of my life.

Because I had been out of the corporate world running a home daycare for the past 10 years, I thought for sure it would take me a long time to find something that I would qualify for, but to my amazement I was hired the first place I applied.

During my hiring interview, I was told that family was important to this company. Approximately three months into my job, the doctor's office called me at work and said they wanted my daughter to see a specialist for a medical problem that she had come down with. I said okay and since we had an HMO, they had to find the doctor and make the appointment. So when her appointment was scheduled for that same afternoon, I went into my boss's office and told her that my daughter had an appointment with a specialist and that it was that afternoon.

My boss replied with "You can go this time, but you will never take off work again to take your kid to the doctor."

I was in disbelief. So much for this company having family values! I walked to my desk, cleared all my personal items and was not coming back after the doctor appointment.

As irate as I was, I had no choice but to go back to work the next day, but only until I could find something else—which, thankfully, within weeks—was a transfer to another department.

Over the past 9+ years I have realized I was not treated any differently from most of her employees, although this person does have her pets. Several people have since been fired or quit due to the company being first and family second.

One girl was fired because she had a scheduled time to enroll her kid in preschool, and this supervisor would not let her take off one hour to do that. So when she took HR's advice to talk to the next person up the corporate ladder, they fired her.

Another girl wanted to take off to be with her dad who was in another state having heart surgery. He was not expected to live. This supervisor told her that she would have to quit in order to get the time off, which she did.

This supervisor lets everyone know that she is active in her church, giving off the perception she is such a good person. She does not have any kids of her own so she is clueless about being a parent, but that does not excuse her actions nor does it excuse her supervisor's actions or HR's inaction.

Shrew bosses are not limited to any location or even to one continent. A gentleman in Australia discovered a shrew boss that had relocated from London.

I was doing my apprenticeship, and my boss was an English expatriate and one of the worst employers I ever had.

I once got paid $20 for 18 hours of over time and had my pay withheld due to the guard dogs getting in to a customer's vehicle that he had told me not to put the window in.

I was constantly bullied, pranked, and fired on the Monday and rehired on the Friday. Thanks to him I changed my career path and now I manage a team of 10 and run a $15 million business.

I pride myself on doing the opposite of what I went through there and have a healthy productive team.

Shrew bosses make their employees' lives miserable. They can also affect the way clients are handled which can risk clients' lifesavings and financial future.

Throughout my career as a financial advisor, I've interacted with quite a few interesting bosses and sales managers in the brokerage, insurance, and banking industries. My worst boss was a guy who was the general agent of a division of a large insurance company who also offered financial planning and investment services.

The GA would make occasional appearances in our sales meetings to motivate the newbies, I among them. He must have been a fan of the classic sales movie, Glengarry Glenn Ross, because his impression of Alec Baldwin's sales manager character was impeccable. He would tell us how he made a million dollars last year, and "I buy a new Cadillac every two years just because I can for cash on the barrel head!"

I was always the guy who had yet another question. I really wanted to fully understand what we were doing so that I could appropriately advise clients. At one point, his exasperation with my pursuit of knowledge of *that which we were selling boiled over. He blasted, "You need to stop worrying about learning and start selling!!"*

I later became the first in the region to actually conduct financial planning for a fee, and I pitched to the GA my idea to create a fee-based department of financial planning within the regional agency and that I'd like to lead it. He invited me to complete a business plan.

I put a ton of work into it and presented him with a 3-ring binder filled with everything from conceptual plans to detailed revenue projections. He accepted physical receipt of the business plan, and then later told me that I wasn't the man to lead the job. His reasoning? I didn't sell enough of the parent company's proprietary insurance products.

Needless to say, I tendered my resignation shortly thereafter.

Shrew bosses either don't understand or don't care that healthy people make great employees, and in order to be healthy, they need to have a good personal—as well as professional—life.

My first boss out of college was an ogre. There's really no nicer way to put it.

A man who became an American citizen, he held no regard for women or for people whose skills were non-technical. A man who was willing to skip all his children's birthdays if necessary, the idea of a personal life was foreign and unwelcome to him. In his opinion, work was more important than anything else in life, and anything that interfered or competed with work was to be cast aside and renounced. He was a tyrant.

He paid us on salary and demanded that we come early and stay late even if the work did not require it. He disregarded my ideas and purposely rejected my work, then criticized me later because I did not fight hard enough for my ideas. When I later did try to fight for my ideas, he ridiculed me by saying my ideas weren't worth fighting for.

Every accomplishment was undercut by the criticism that it was not enough, and every failure was displayed proudly as proof of how inept I was.

I was so belittled and intimidated at work that I began having trouble sleeping and had anxiety attacks whenever my boss entered the office. The last straw came when he told me I needed to get rid of my puppy so I could focus on work more. He also told me I needed to quit blogging on my personal time as well, because it might interfere with my focus. He basically gave me a choice between this work hell and my puppy and blog (both of which were the only things helping me cope with my job) so I told him I'd made my choice and quit.

It was the best decision I've ever made and I've never looked back.

Shrew bosses don't need a reason to display their despicable characteristics. They act like a shrew simply because they are a shrew boss.

I worked at a pizza place when I was in college. It was not a chain and the owner was there every day.

The owner had a temper, and you learned to duck. When he got REALLY mad he would fire somebody. It didn't matter what he was angry with. He could have stubbed his toe, somebody was going down. Then he would hire them back a few days later. I worked there for three years and got fired 9 times.

Oh, I can hear you out there. "Why would you go back?" It was the early 80s. Inflation was high and jobs were scarce—especially the part time jobs in college towns.

If you're dealing with a shrew boss, they may or may not attack with deadly force. A shrew boss can simply wear you down so you die the proverbial death of a thousand cuts.

It is hard to confront a shrew boss, because no single incident may stand out. It is simply that the overall attitude and demeanor makes it impossible for their team to thrive.

Often, you can politely ask a shrew boss a simple question: "When you do or say..., I feel demeaned, devalued, and hurt. Is this what you intend?"

If they are the type of shrew boss that doesn't care about anyone, and they are simply acting out of their natural instincts, there's nothing that you can do but seek greener pastures. On the other hand, if a shrew boss is unaware of their own behavior or has become desensitized to it over time, powerful change can become possible.

The Shrew

CHAPTER TWENTY

The Taming of the Zoo

Wild animals can be exotic, beautiful, and exciting if you know how to handle them. Otherwise, they can be dangerous and deadly.

Work is an important part of our lives. Oftentimes, people forget that being productive is an essential element of happiness.

When inmates in prison behave well, they are given privileges. One of the privileges these inmates can receive is the right to work.

Too many people in the world today have put themselves in a position where they are enslaved to their work and, therefore, enslaved to a worst boss. I have studied the diaries of slaves and slave owners that lived in America in the 19th Century. Most slaves had the means to escape the slave owner at virtually any time. What kept them enslaved to their master was the fact that both they and the slave owner knew that escaped slaves did not have the ability to take care of themselves and their families.

Far too many workers here in the twenty-first century are enslaved to worst bosses simply because they do not have the wherewithal to take care of themselves or their families, even for a brief period of time, until they find another job. The chains they feel are just as real and confining as the chains worn by slaves in the nineteenth century.

My fervent hope is that you will consider this book and the stories in it as your own emancipation proclamation. If so, you can begin today to escape your worst boss environment by changing it or making plans to move on.

We spend too much of our lives working not to feel productive, appreciated and fulfilled. Your work life is much like raising children in that there may be single incidences that are uncomfortable or unpleasant, but overall the experience should be among the most rewarding parts of your life.

Regardless of whether you have your dream job, you're currently dealing with a worst boss, or you've declared your emancipation and you are preparing to escape to the Promised Land, it is imperative that you have an emergency fund. The lack of a simple cash reserve of six months' worth of your living expenses can keep you enslaved for life. This emergency fund, along with an updated resume and keeping your network of contacts current, will make you worst-boss-proof or at least worst-boss-resistant.

Work is not always fun. That's why they don't call it play. There are certain tasks that must be done as a part of any job, and not all of them are pleasant all the time; however, if you can't step back and examine your overall career—finding it to be everything you want to get out of your professional life—you've got to make a change or leave. You really have nothing to lose, because you're enslaved to a worst boss now. You must vow to improve the situation or move on.

It is important to know what you would like your career to look and feel like.

I have the privilege of traveling across the country and around the world to do speaking and consulting for countless corporations. When I meet disgruntled employees who are being victimized by worst bosses, I often ask them to tell me what their perfect job or career would look like. Unfortunately, many of these people are so bogged down in the slavery of their worst boss environment, they are simply trying to survive day to day, and they have never thought about creating their wish list.

Before you make any moves or changes, clearly understand what it is that you want. You can't hit a target you don't have.

When you attempt to confront your worst boss with the intent of making change within your work environment, it is critical that you approach them with the respect that they deserve. Worst bosses are often despicable human beings that are hard to respect, but if you are involved in an organization that you care about, you should at least respect your boss's position.

While president, Harry Truman was being criticized for his performance and was being treated disrespectfully by a certain constituency. He confronted them stating, "I don't care what you think about Harry Truman, but I do care what you think about the President of the United States and will require you to respect the office." Your boss's position deserves your respect even if, as a person, they haven't earned your respect.

When you confront any of the worst bosses that have been described in the real-life stories throughout this book, be respectful of their position and document your situation. If you get emotional or discuss your feelings, you will lose before you even get into the starting gate. If you get into a "he-said-she-said" argument with your worst boss without documentation, you will inevitably lose the argument.

Never return bad behavior to your worst boss in exchange for the bad behavior they have shown you. You must do unto your boss as you would have them do unto you. This will not always meet with success, but without it, you don't have a chance.

In any discussion with your worst boss, part of the conversation must deal with your own behavior, asking: "What can I do here to be a more valuable employee?"; "How can I be of more service to you as my boss?"; or "What milestones do you feel I should focus upon to improve my value to the organization?"

Even if you're dealing with the most egregious worst boss, you must be willing to be responsible for part of the change that is necessary.

Far too many people have never considered their career as something that was a matter of choice. They feel trapped and stifled.

Begin to ask yourself the following questions:

1. Why do I work where I do?
2. Am I happy and fulfilled today?
3. What would I do, career-wise, if money were no object?
4. When I look back over my 40- or 50-year career someday, what do I want to have accomplished?

Most people have never considered a career outside of their field or a job outside of their area. The world is a huge place, and new opportunities are being born every day. There are people making a wonderful living doing things that make them happy within jobs and careers that you have never even heard of or thought about.

Expand your mind and your horizons relating to your career. Once you have seen the Promised Land and dreamed of freedom, slavery will become intolerable.

If you will vow to make this change, your worst boss may turn out to be the best friend you ever had, because he or she will be the catalyst for positive change in your professional life.